Marion Bridge

Revised Edition

Daniel MacIvor

Talonbooks
Vancouver

Talonbooks
P.O. Box 2076, Vancouver, British Columbia, Canada V6B 3S3
www.talonbooks.com

Typeset in New Baskerville and printed and bound in Canada.

First Revised Printing: 2006

The publisher gratefully acknowledges the financial support of the Canada Council for the Arts; the Government of Canada through the Book Publishing Industry Development Program; and the Province of British Columbia through the British Columbia Arts Council for our publishing activities.

LIBRARY AND ARCHIVES CANADA CATALOGUING IN PUBLICATION

MacIvor, Daniel, 1962–
    Marion Bridge / Daniel MacIvor. – Rev. ed.

A play.
ISBN-13: 978-0-88922-552-7
ISBN-10: 0-88922-552-4

    I. Title.

PS8575.I86M37 2006   C812'.54   C2006-903440-0

For my Mother

Contents

Foreword

I wanted to write a brilliant screenplay. I tried for years to write a brilliant screenplay but it wasn't happening. I decided the reason why I wasn't writing a brilliant screenplay was because the universe of the screenplay was too broad. I've always been structuralist. I work inside the specific limitations of the theatre which is a time-based medium, centred on sharing DNA between the audience and the performer. A medium with very specific requirements. The cinema was an open thing, anything was possible. In the cinema you want a mountain? Here's a mountain. In the theatre a mountain is a sound and a particular quality of light. The theatre is limited by reality. The reality of cinema is the truth of light projected on a flat surface. Something that once happened. Nostalgia. I only understood the immediate. Movement in physical space. Something happening now. So how was I to write a brilliant screenplay? I had no idea. I decided my best bet was to write a play and then to base the screenplay on the play. The play would be the finite universe within which I could find the words for a movie. That play was *Marion Bridge*.

I approached Emmy Alcorn at Mulgrave Road Theatre in Guysborough, Nova Scotia with an idea and she commissioned the play. I wrote the first draft in the offices of Mulgrave Road in the spring of 1997. Other than the usual writing anguish it was a relatively painless experience, it was a simple story and the characters came easily, early on it was clear that the characters were running the show. I was happy with that. And as usual I knew the actresses I would be using in the play and so I to some extent tailored the characters to what I saw as the performers' particular strengths. The play premiered and was a great success on its Nova Scotia tour. Oddly some critics were saying it was my strongest work yet. This surprised me for a couple of reasons. First, it was so different than the other work I had done; it was both more narratively straightforward and more sentimental than the theatre I had been making. Also, the play was, in my mind at the time, just a step toward the film it would one day be. In retrospect perhaps that's what helped the play realize itself, I was not so concerned about writing a great play, I was trying to write a great screenplay. It took the heat off the play, and the play appreciated the absence of my ego.

Later that year I finished the first draft of the screenplay. Originally I was going to direct the film myself, it would have been my first feature film. But when I showed it to some Toronto producers they said, knowing my theatre work, that it wasn't "MacIvor enough." This was an immediate red flag for me, I suspected I was going to get this kind of response from any Canadian producer I approached, and it was a conversation I did not want to enter. What was "MacIvor"? I wrote it, wasn't that me enough? I learned early on that to "try" and be oneself was antithetical to being oneself. I saw a lot of existential angst and self-consciousness in my future. In the interim I had given the script to my roommate and brilliant editor/aspiring director Wiebke von Carlsfeld thinking that she might edit the film. She responded so strongly to the script than when I tried to consider another director Wiebke was the only person who came into my mind. Once Wiebke took on the project it was up to her to find producers, which she easily did. Suddenly the project was a go and I had to dig into the script for re-writes. It quickly became very clear to me that this was going to be a different process altogether. I'm not sure when things began to radically change, in the world of film there are so many readers, so many notes, so many demands, so many people to please, it's hard to keep track of whose suggestions I followed and whose I ignored. I had already made some major changes in the story. The first was changing the character of Theresa from a nun in a crisis of faith to an abandoned wife. As I tried to write a nun for film the script demanded to know why she was a nun. In the theatre, since the audience is watching a live person in real time they don't ask the same questions, along with the suspension of their disbelief comes a trust in the performance: "She says she's a nun, she acts like a nun, she's a nun." They are active viewers, their belief makes the story true. In the cinema the passive viewer needs more information, they ask questions about back-story and motivation that need to be addressed. I was not interested in why Theresa was a nun, it wasn't part of the story for me, and so I ditched the nun and gave the audience something they would more readily understand, a jilted wife. This worked for me since in some ways Theresa felt abandoned by her God, her husband as it were. The next major change was the casting of Molly Parker as the oldest sister Agnes. Molly was a good friend of both Wiebke's and mine. She had been in Wiebke's short film *From Morning On I Waited Yesterday* and we had played opposite one another in Don McKellar's TV series *Twitch City*, she was both a powerful and delicate actress—as well a lovely person—and would be perfect for the project—but for her age. There was no way that Molly would be the eldest sister of a trio, unless the others were teenagers, and that was not going to work. So Agnes became the youngest sister, which altered the dynamic of the three in many subtle yet profound ways. Then came the rest of the cast, the stunning Rebecca Jenkins as Theresa and the excellent Stacey Smith had the ideal qualities for the lovely oddball Louise. Everything seemed to be working. But there was something that wasn't right. I had many notes about "not enough happens" in the script—indeed, regardless of how many tiny catastrophes I have in my film scripts that is a complaint I am forever hearing—in the theatre I concern myself with what I call the sublime banal—the microcosms, the personal. That stuff doesn't sell to producers on this side of the Atlantic. At the same time I felt they were right, something seemed slight about the story. I decided to change the central act of Agnes having been forced to abandon her infant child, Joanie, due to pressure around ideas of religious piety and what-would-the-neighbours-think. Instead Joanie was born out of a sexually abusive relationship with Agnes's own father. It took us awhile to sell Wiebke on this change but in the end she saw how it made the central questions about why a woman—even a girl—who wanted a child would allow the child to be taken away. Incorporating this change shifted the very theme of the story. In the play *Marion Bridge* the theme, the title even, refers to how we remember things. In the screenplay Marion Bridge is the name Agnes and her sisters had imagined giving to the unborn Joanie, it refers to the wonderful thing we never manage to own. And I think it was this change that in the end created two very different stories. Of course there were other changes between the actual screenplay and the film that ended up being made, many of these came from purely practical concerns. One major cut was the sequence of scenes where Agnes picks up and fucks the businessman in the hotel bar. Both Wiebke and I felt that this was a very important series of scenes to show Agnes's struggle to have some kind of power by using sex as a tool. However, running out of time and money during the shoot, it became necessary to cut these scenes, something Wiebke and I still both feel sorry about. But these are the realities of independent filmmaking.

In the end it's strange how I feel that the play I wrote in order to write the screenplay is really the stronger of the two scripts. This is not to take anything away from the film, Wiebke did a marvelous job and it has played around the world winning awards and thrilling critics and audiences alike. And as well, the unseen characters in the play are forever in my mind cast as the actors from the film, Marguerite MacNeil will forever be Rose the mother and Ellen Page is Joanie no matter how many times I watch the play again. I suppose that these feelings really speak to the fact that I am more a man of the theatre than a filmmaker. I haven't watched the film again in years and yet I continue to direct and re-write productions of the play. The screenplay is something that once happened while the play is still a living, breathing, present thing in my life.

I am thrilled to have the opportunity to have both of these scripts published together in a volume. It speaks directly to how these two mediums deal with story and how film affects word. I was once told that a brilliant film could be watched with the sound turned down and the audience would still get the story. Perhaps that's true, perhaps it's impossible to write a brilliant screenplay, maybe it's up to people to make brilliant movies, maybe the script is just something for people to talk about. I guess it's up to you to be the judge.

Daniel MacIvor
June 12, 2006
Halifax, Nova Scotia

MARION BRIDGE

The Play

Marion Bridge was commissioned and first produced in September 1998 by Mulgrave Road Theatre, in association with da da kamera, in Guysborough, Nova Scotia with the following cast:

AGNES . . . . Jenny Munday
THERESA. . . . . Mary Ellen MacLean
LOUISE . . . . Emmy Alcorn
Voice of JUSTIN . . . . John Dartt
Voice of KARA . . . . Janet MacLellan

Directed by Josephine Le Grice
Lighting by Leigh Ann Vardy
Set and Costumes by Janet MacLellan
Stage Manager: Judy Joe

Characters

AGNES MACKEIGAN: The eldest sister, 30s–40s, an actress/waitress living in Toronto.

THERESA MACKEIGAN: The middle sister, 30s–40s, a nun living in a farming order in New Brunswick.

LOUISE MACKEIGAN: The youngest sister, 30s, lives at home on Cape Breton Island

Setting

All of the action (with the exception of the last scene) takes place in the kitchen of the family home. The last scene takes place on the bank of a river.

Sound

It is essential that the television sound come from a speaker placed in the offstage area where the television is indicated. It would be unfortunate to have the television sound coming through the main theatre speakers.

ACT ONE

Scene 1

AGNES sits alone on stage. A flask in her bag; a suitcase beside her. She addresses the audience.

AGNES: In the dream I'm drowning. But I don't know it at first. At first I hear water and I imagine it's going to be a lovely dream. Even though every time I dream the dream I'm drowning each and every time I dream the dream I forget. Fooled by the sound of water I guess and I imagine it's a dream of a wonderful night on the beach, or a cruise in the moonlight, or an August afternoon in a secret cove—but a moment after having been fooled into expecting bonfires or handsome captains or treasures in the weedy shore it becomes very clear that the water I'm hearing is the water that's rushing around my ears and fighting its way into my mouth and pulling me down into its dark, soggy oblivion. No captains, no treasures, no bonfires for me, no in my dream I'm drowning. And then, just when it seems it's over—that I drown and that's the dream—in the distance, on the beach, I see a child. A tall thin child, maybe nine or ten. And his sister, younger, five. Then behind them comes their mother spreading out a blanket on the sand. It's a picnic. And beside the mother is the man. Tall. Strong. And broad shoulders, good for sitting on if you're five, or even ten. Good for leaning on if you're tired, good for crying on if you're sad. And he's got his hands on his hips and he's looking out at the water, and he sees something. Me. And he reaches out and touches his wife's elbow who at that very moment sees something too and then the children, as if they're still connected to their mother's eyes, think they might see the same thing. And with all my strength—if you can call strength that strange, desperate, exhausted panic—I wave. My right arm. High. So they'll be sure to see. And they do. They see me. And then all of them, standing in a perfect line, they all wave back. The little girl, her brother, their mother and the man. They smile and wave. Then the mother returns to her blanket and the basket of food she has there, the man sits, stretching out his legs, propping himself up on one arm, the little boy runs off in search of starfish or crab shells and the little girl smiles and waves, smiles and waves and smiles and waves. And then I drown. And that's so disturbing, because you know what they say when you die in your dream. Strange. But stranger I guess is that I'm still here. Back here. Still here.

THERESA enters.

THERESA: Why are you sitting in the dark?

AGNES: I like the dark, it's good for my complexion.

THERESA: I thought you were going to have a nap.

AGNES: Whatever.

THERESA exits briefly to turn on some lights.

THERESA: "Whatever." Don't give me any of your Toronto talk.

AGNES: Toronto talk? "Whatever" is not Toronto talk. It's a word. It's in the dictionary. Look it up.

The following dialogue overlaps slightly, enough to indicate they aren't really listening to one another.

THERESA: "Whatever." "Whatever."

AGNES: If there even is a dictionary here.

THERESA: What's "whatever" supposed to mean?

AGNES: The only book I ever remember seeing around here is the Bible.

THERESA: That's all you hear from the kids— "whatever"—and all that means is "who cares" or "I don't care." What kind of world is that?

AGNES: There's probably no dictionary here because I bet the Bible doesn't allow good Christians to have dictionaries. Too much information.

THERESA: Nobody cares, that's why the world is in the mess it is. The whole world's gone "whatever."

AGNES: Whatever.

A beat.

THERESA: How's everything here?

AGNES: Fine. Where did you rush off to?

THERESA: I told you. Mass.

AGNES: On Friday night? What, are you gunning for Nun of the Month?

THERESA: Father Dave was on, he always does a nice sermon. *(noticing the suitcase)* Have you not been upstairs?

AGNES: I'm steeling myself for the journey.

THERESA picks up the suitcase and moves to exit.

THERESA: I'm in with Louise and you'll be in the little
blue room. I was going to move Mother downstairs
and put you in her room but she wouldn't have it.
She wants her view.

AGNES: It's got wheels.

THERESA: What?

AGNES: The suitcase has wheels.

THERESA: Oh I'm fine.

AGNES: It's got wheels.

THERESA: I don't mind carrying it.

AGNES: Use the bloody wheels! It's not a sin you know.
You don't have to make every goddamn thing you do
the way of the cross.

THERESA: Are you drunk?

AGNES: Drunk? What exactly is drunk?

THERESA exits.

AGNES: *(off to THERESA)* Is drunk measured by amount
drunk or by the effects of the drinking? And anyway a
lady never gets drunk a lady just relaxes. Loose
women get drunk. And God knows I'm not a loose
woman. Not that I haven't tried. But am I relaxed? I
might be too relaxed to know. If I'm relaxed. Or not.
What's relaxed? I can't really answer that question.
But I could try to tell you how I feel; if I felt anything.
And I don't think I've felt anything in some time, now
that I think of it. And I'm not feeling anything right
now, certainly not relaxed. Not anything. But no pain
either, and isn't that what they say, "Feeling no pain"?

So yes maybe I am drunk. But I think "drunk" is supposed to be a lot more fun than this isn't it? But then again why am I asking you? You've never been drunk have you? You've never been anything other than a saint, have you Sister Theresa?

THERESA returns.

THERESA: Mother's up.

AGNES: Mmmm.

THERESA: If you want to see her.

AGNES: I saw her.

THERESA: Oh.

AGNES: She was asleep.

THERESA: The pills put her right out.

AGNES: Mmmm.

THERESA: But she's up now. If you want to see her.

AGNES: Stop with the "If you want to see her"—of course I want to see her. What do you think I came here for? Not a bloody holiday that's for sure.

THERESA: Well I just—

AGNES: Don't pull any of your passive-aggressive bullshit on me, Saint Theresa.

THERESA: Pardon me?

AGNES: (*mocking her*) "Mother's up if you want to see her." A slight emotional tremor in the voice—eyes slightly averted—fingers nervously picking at her skirt. I'll see her when I'm goddamn ready. Christ.

THERESA: As you wish.

AGNES: First of all there's no one to meet me, then I've got to take the bus in from the airport—which alone and with luggage is a serious exercise in humility—then I'm not home fifteen minutes and you're rushing off to Mass and leave me alone here with Mother on her death bed.

THERESA: Oh stop it.

AGNES: Why do I let you do this to me?

THERESA: Whatever's being done to you you're doing it to yourself.

AGNES: There she bloody goes again.

THERESA: Louise is home.

AGNES: What?

THERESA: She just pulled in.

AGNES: Oh fantastic, now that you've got me in a state.

AGNES exits.

AGNES: Christ bloody hell. Christly goddamn bloody hell.

THERESA: Just calm down.

LOUISE enters. She holds a can of Pepsi throughout the scene.

LOUISE: How's Mother?

THERESA: A little restless.

LOUISE: Agnes get in alright?

THERESA: Yes fine.

LOUISE: Where is she?

THERESA: In the bathroom. So you got the car all taken care of?

LOUISE: Oh yeah, it was just some buildup in the fuel line.

Pause.

LOUISE: She drunk?

THERESA: Well she hates to fly.

LOUISE: Mmmm.

THERESA: She's a little upset.

LOUISE: 'Cause of Mother?

THERESA: I don't think Agnes thought she'd be quite so bad.

LOUISE: She went in?

THERESA: Apparently. Not while I was here.

LOUISE: Did Mother get her pills?

THERESA: Yes.

AGNES: (*calling from off*) Who's that I hear?

AGNES enters.

LOUISE: Hi.

AGNES: Oh God! Look at you! You cut your hair.

LOUISE: It's just the same.

AGNES: It really suits you.

LOUISE: Sorry I didn't pick you up but the car's been giving me some trouble.

AGNES: Oh that's alright, I love a nice bus ride.

LOUISE: How you doing Agnes?

AGNES: Wonderful. Just wonderful. I got involved with a little repertory company this winter. They do these challenging little adaptations of Ibsen and Chekhov

and Strindberg and so on—really interesting stuff—
tart them up a bit, you know, the girls in black vinyl
boots and big hair styles and the boys in little Speedo
bathing suits, that sort of thing. Audiences just eat it
up. And a really interesting take on the plays too, not
just all flash and so on, a brilliant, brilliant director
working with the company, really challenging man,
really sharp mind. And a little film work, small things
but good parts, nothing too gaudy—the problem with
leads is that the supporting parts are so much better.
Last week my agent sent me out for a second lead in a
cable M.O.W. and honestly! I'm glad I didn't get it. I
wouldn't have been able to hold my head up when
the press came out. But me me me enough about me,
how are you honey. Tell me everything. What's going
on with you? How are you?

LOUISE: Good.

   Pause.

LOUISE: Anyway I'm going to go have a minute with
Mother.

AGNES: Yes and then we'll sit down and have a nice long
chat.

   LOUISE exits.

AGNES: My God what happened to her? Did she get a
shock or something?

THERESA: What do you mean?

AGNES: She looks terrible, all puffy and strange.

THERESA: She's fine, she's just herself. She's worried
about Mother.

AGNES: So you admit she seems strange.

THERESA: Agnes, she is strange. She's always been strange. I don't know what you expect—everything's just the same as ever: Louise is strange, I'm running the show and you're drunk. Same as it ever was except Mother's dying. Alright?

AGNES: Alright.

Silence.

THERESA: I've been here a week, it feels like a month.

AGNES: Will you have a drink with me?

THERESA: No thank you.

AGNES: I hate to drink alone.

THERESA: When have you known me to drink?

AGNES: There's always Mother.

THERESA: Don't! Don't you dare. And she'll ask too. She wouldn't ask me but she'd ask you. But don't. It's very dangerous with the medication she's on.

AGNES: I thought she couldn't talk.

THERESA: She can't. Once it got into her thingy ... her larynx or whatsit she could only make these little squeaks but now there's no sound at all. That's why there's these.

> *THERESA removes a bunch of yellow Post-it notes from her pocket. She shows them one by one to AGNES.*

THERESA: She's got all these various things she writes down. For "yes" she writes a circle and for "no" it's just a slash like this. If she wants a cup of tea she makes a "k."

AGNES: A "k"?

THERESA: For "kettle." A big "H" means she's hungry and if she writes a little "h" that's for Sandy.

AGNES: Sandy?

THERESA: It looks like a little "h" but really it's a chair, because Sandy sits in the little chair when he comes over to read to her.

AGNES: Sandy comes over?

THERESA: He reads to her.

AGNES: How is he?

THERESA: I haven't seen him myself, this is all from Louise I'm getting this. And don't throw the notes out. Louise likes to save them.

AGNES: I bet he's fat now.

THERESA: Sandy? No!

AGNES: I thought you didn't see him.

THERESA: I didn't but Sandy was always taking such care of himself. With his hair and his clothes all nice and just so.

AGNES: Fat and bald.

THERESA: That sounds less like a prediction and more like a wish.

AGNES: I've got no feelings for Sandy Deveau.

THERESA: A squiggle like this means she has a headache—don't ask me why but evidently that's the story. Just give her a Tylenol—along with the regular morphine. And a squiggle like this just rip up the paper. I got this one a couple of times. It means she wants a cigarette.

AGNES: She's not smoking?

THERESA: She's only got half a lung.

AGNES: Even less reason for her to quit.

THERESA: No.

AGNES: Oh come on let her have a cigarette.

THERESA: No. It's a sin. No, it's a crime. And if sin doesn't mean anything anymore well crime still does. Period. Alright. Oh, and if she makes a dot, just a dot … like that, that means she's got an itch. And sometimes … I don't have one here, but sometimes if she's feeling all soft and lovey she'll make a little heart. She hasn't been doing too many of those. And "P" is for pee.

AGNES: For what?

THERESA: Pee.

AGNES: "P" for what?

THERESA: Pee, pee just pee, go PEE.

AGNES: Oh.

THERESA: And if she gives you a "P" … well we'll get into that later.

AGNES: She's not going to be giving me any "P."

THERESA: Oh yes she will.

AGNES: No, I'm telling you she won't be because I'm not doing that. I'm not a nurse.

THERESA: Well neither am I, neither's Louise, but we still have to do it.

AGNES: We'll get a real nurse.

THERESA: She doesn't want a nurse.

AGNES: Don't be ridiculous.

THERESA: We'll talk about this in the morning.

AGNES: Talk all you want.

LOUISE enters.

LOUISE: Mother says you haven't been in to see her.

AGNES: I was in.

LOUISE: She says you weren't.

AGNES: I'll spend the day with her tomorrow.

LOUISE hands a note to THERESA.

LOUISE: Here.

THERESA looks at the note. She places it in her pocket.

THERESA: Mmm.

LOUISE moves to exit.

AGNES: Now where are you going? You sit down here with me.

LOUISE: After. My show's on.

AGNES: Forget your stupid old show! Sit down!

LOUISE: For a minute.

AGNES: So, now talk to me.

Pause.

AGNES: Will you have a drink?

LOUISE: I got a Pepsi.

Pause.

AGNES: So. Are you working?

LOUISE: I got a job at the Red Rooster in November.

AGNES: Right, right, that restaurant.

LOUISE: Pub.

AGNES: Pub. How's that going?

LOUISE: I got laid off in January.

THERESA: I didn't like that place anyway.

LOUISE: You were only there once.

THERESA: And what a night that was.

LOUISE: The Christmas party.

THERESA: Mother and I down in that ... what was it a cellar or something. Dark! And loud! A fellow in a Santa suit with an accordion this far from my ear. Of course Mother was in her glory.

LOUISE: She did an excellent karaoke.

THERESA: My dear heavens. And the way she was carrying on with Santa Claus.

LOUISE: He started it.

THERESA: Well she's the one who tried to pull off his beard.

LOUISE: I know, and it was real.

AGNES: Sounds charming. I'm so sorry I missed it. So Sandy's been by.

LOUISE: Now and then.

AGNES: How is he?

LOUISE: Just the same.

THERESA: She wants to know what he looks like.

LOUISE: Just the same.

AGNES: (*to THERESA*) No I don't. (*to LOUISE*) How's his friend?

LOUISE: Who?

AGNES: Charles or whatever.

LOUISE: Oh Charlie. Oh Charlie's, you know, just the same.

AGNES: Do they still have the restaurant?

LOUISE: Naw, closed that down. They opened up a gas station.

AGNES: A gas station?!

LOUISE: Sandy said people don't go out to restaurants anymore because they eat home.

THERESA: Tell her the end of it.

LOUISE: The end of it?

THERESA: The end of it. That Sandy said.

LOUISE: Oh yeah, he goes: people don't go out to restaurants anymore because they eat home but you can't get gas home—and then he goes: unless your mother's cooking.

THERESA and LOUISE laugh.

LOUISE: But that was Charlie said that not Sandy. And you know what else!

THERESA: What?

LOUISE: He's over here, Sandy is, the other week and he's after me to join this bowling team they've got going.

AGNES: Bowling?

LOUISE: Imagine me bowling. That would be a laugh, me bowling.

THERESA: It would be good for you to get out a bit more.

LOUISE: I'm not joining any bowling team. Especially because they play on Wednesdays and my show's on Wednesdays.

THERESA: I thought your show was on tonight.

LOUISE: I have several shows.

AGNES: Louise!

LOUISE: What?

AGNES: Look at yourself.

LOUISE: What?

AGNES: What are you doing with yourself?

LOUISE: Nothing.

AGNES: Tell me something, tell me something new. What's happening? What's going on?

LOUISE: With who?

AGNES: With you.

LOUISE: I don't know.

AGNES: Well … what are you thinking about these days? You must be thinking about something.

>   *Pause.*

LOUISE: Um.

AGNES: What are you thinking about?

THERESA: Agnes …

AGNES: Louise? What are you thinking about?

>   *Pause.*

LOUISE: *Ryan's Cove.*

AGNES: Where's that?

LOUISE: On TV. It started five minutes ago, that's why I'm thinking about it. It's going to be good too. 'Cause last week Mrs. Ryan found out she had oil on this land she got left by this young guy Jake she was married to for a couple of weeks who she really truly loved but who died. And she doesn't want her daughter Kara to know that there's oil on the land 'cause Kara'd just sell it for the money. Mrs. Ryan doesn't want to sell it 'cause it's her only memory of Jake. See, Kara's really evil, right. Her boyfriend is Justin and he's really good, but Kara's just plain evil. You're supposed to feel sorry for her because she's confused and has trouble with men. I don't feel sorry for her though. And now Kara knows that Justin has a gun, but Justin doesn't know he has a gun because he got it when he robbed the bank after he got hypnotized by Earl's cousin. Earl's cousin's not on the show anymore. They made him mean, and then they made him nice, and then they killed him in a car crash. Earl's cousin was really Earl, they had the same guy as both of them because they were supposed to be identical cousins— which I never heard of. Did you ever hear of that, identical cousins?

THERESA: Not really, no.

LOUISE: Ah, they make half that stuff up I think.

Pause.

LOUISE: Is our talk done?

AGNES: Sure.

LOUISE moves to exit.

LOUISE: It's going to be good, you want to watch it?

AGNES: Maybe later.

LOUISE exits. Pause.

THERESA: Come on in and spend a little time with Mother.

AGNES: No. Not tonight.

THERESA: When then?

AGNES: Not tonight.

THERESA: As you wish.

> *THERESA exits. We hear recorded voices from a television program LOUISE switches on off stage:*

JUSTIN: "Good Lord Kara where did you get that gun?"

KARA: "It's not my gun Justin. It's yours."

JUSTIN: "That's impossible."

KARA: "See. Look. The registration is in your name."

JUSTIN: "My God Kara we've got to get rid of it."

KARA: "No! I have plans for this."

JUSTIN: "Kara what are you thinking? Are you insane?!"

KARA: "No Justin I'm not insane. I'm just bad. Born bad. Bad to the bone."

> *Alone on stage AGNES lifts her right arm high and waves. The light fades.*

Scene 2

Mid-afternoon the next day. THERESA crosses the stage carrying clean sheets. LOUISE is off stage in the living room watching a daytime talk show which we can hear. AGNES enters with shopping bags and a bouquet of flowers.

AGNES: I give up! I honestly give up! I surrender to this town, I surrender, I give up! Look at these.

She heads toward the living room.

AGNES: Look at these.

She exits into the living room.

AGNES: (*off*) Look at these!

LOUISE: (*off*) What?

AGNES: (*off*) Aren't they sad!

LOUISE: (*off*) Yeah.

AGNES re-enters. Throughout the following she exits and returns with water in a pitcher for the flowers.

AGNES: (*off to LOUISE*) I marched all over town—and you wouldn't believe what they try to pass off as flower shops! Two stores didn't have a live flower in the place, just some God-awful arrangements of fake silk and feathers. And finally I find a place that has live flowers and this is what they give me! Have you ever seen such a sad affair! At home there are flower shops on every block, and tulips with heads as big as your fist. And this? This is two bouquets—I had her put two together to make this scrawny little thing—imagine trying to pass off a bit of hay and some wild flowers from the ditch as a bouquet. What I was really looking for was something special, something exotic. They don't get much more exotic here than those boring old African Violets—I asked the girl about Birds of Paradise and she recommended the pet store! Poor stunned little thing—ah well it's not her fault she hasn't been off this damn island her whole life.

THERESA enters.

AGNES: (*off to LOUISE*) And wait 'til you hear about my adventures trying to find wheat-free bread.

THERESA: What are those for?

AGNES: For Mother's room. Do you want to bring them in?

THERESA: Oh.

AGNES: What?

THERESA: Mother doesn't like cut flowers.

AGNES: What?

THERESA: Oh yes, every time I ever tried to bring her flowers she'd get all sad because she didn't like to see them cut—she thought they should be left to grow.

AGNES: I've brought her flowers before.

THERESA: I know what—I know a place you can get gorgeous little pots of African Violets. She'd love that.

AGNES: Christ.

THERESA: And while we're on harping at you—because I know that's what you're going to think this is—

AGNES: Oh I can't wait!

THERESA: —and I know you don't like to be told what to do—

AGNES: What?

THERESA: Well …

AGNES: I should watch my language?

THERESA: Actually, yes.

AGNES: You're kidding? What did I say?

THERESA: You don't know?

AGNES: No, what?

THERESA: The "c" word.

AGNES: The "c" word? No I certainly have not used the "c" word here!

THERESA: Yes you … Oh! No, not that "c" word. Good heavens.

AGNES: Well which "c" word, there's only one "c" word … Oh well I guess that's a "c" word too but I don't think I've had any cause to say that here either.

THERESA: The Lord's name.

AGNES: Jesus!

THERESA: Agnes.

AGNES: So it's like that is it Sister?

THERESA: It's not me—it's Louise. It bothers her.

AGNES: Louise?

THERESA: She started going to a prayer group. She takes it very seriously.

AGNES: Louise?

THERESA: She likes the people—and it's good she gets out. And I don't care what you believe or don't believe but prayer never hurt anyone.

AGNES: So you've got poor Louise in the pack now.

THERESA: It had nothing to do with me. It was her decision.

AGNES: Next thing you know she'll be joining up with your Sisters of Saint E-I-E-I-O or whatever it is.

THERESA: It's a little early for this isn't it? Or are you just getting going?

AGNES: It's easy to hide away—what's hard is living a real life.

THERESA: Oh just have another drink.

AGNES: I had a half and a gla—a glass and a half of wine with lunch and that's—What the hell am I explaining myself to you for? Christ!

> *Silence.*

THERESA: Are you going to bring those flowers in to Mother?

AGNES: I thought they'd just upset her.

THERESA: They're very nice.

AGNES: They're not very nice. I'll leave them here.

THERESA: You've got to go in sometime.

AGNES: God that television! (*yelling off*) Louise would you turn that off!

LOUISE: (*off*) I'm watching it.

AGNES: (*yelling off*) Well mute it or something.

LOUISE: (*off*) What?

THERESA: Here we go.

> *THERESA exits.*

AGNES: (*yelling off*) Mute it!

LOUISE: (*off*) Mute it? It's a talk show! You can't mute a talk show!

AGNES: (*yelling off*) Listen to some music or something!

LOUISE: (*off*) It's my show!

AGNES exits to LOUISE.

AGNES: (*off*) We just need a bit of a break alright.

The television is shut off.

LOUISE: (*off*) Hey!

AGNES enters with the remote control. LOUISE follows close behind.

AGNES: I'm calling a time-out on the TV.

LOUISE: Give me that back. It's my TV.

AGNES: And it's my headache.

LOUISE: Maybe you wouldn't have a headache if you weren't up all night drinking.

AGNES: I was up all night because I couldn't sleep!

LOUISE: You were up all night because it took you that long to drink the whole bottle of Mother's arthritis brandy.

AGNES: Get off my back.

LOUISE: You drink so much it makes you stupid—and if you're not drinking it makes you sick—and if you're not sick or stupid, you're cranky. What's the fun of that anyway?

AGNES: I guess I'd be better off sitting in front of the TV all my life.

LOUISE: Maybe you would be. Gimme that.

AGNES: No.

LOUISE: It's mine, gimme it.

AGNES: Forget it.

LOUISE: You can't tell me what to do.

AGNES: Yes I can.

LOUISE: No you can't.

AGNES: Just watch me.

> *THERESA enters.*

THERESA: Please! Keep it down.

LOUISE: (*to THERESA*) Tell her she can't tell me what to do.

THERESA: Look, Louise, look let's just … sit down.

LOUISE: Yeah I'll sit down, in front of my show.

THERESA: Sit down.

LOUISE: No.

THERESA: There's something we have to talk about.

LOUISE: No. What?

> *THERESA takes out the note LOUISE gave her last night. Pause. LOUISE sits.*

AGNES: What's that?

THERESA: It's a note from Mother.

AGNES: Yes. So? What does it say?

> *THERESA gives AGNES the note. AGNES looks at it for a moment.*

AGNES: What is it? A "B"? What's a "B" for?

THERESA: Bradley.

AGNES: Bradley?

LOUISE: (*helpfully to* AGNES) Dad.

AGNES: (*to* LOUISE) I know. (*to* THERESA) What about him?

THERESA: Mother wants us to see him, the three of us.

AGNES: You're not serious.

THERESA: She wants us all to make amends.

AGNES: Make amends? Make amends of what? I'm not seeing him.

LOUISE: Kara Ryan's father came back from living in France for ten years and she saw him …

THERESA: Mother wants us to.

AGNES: What good will it do her for us to see that bastard?

THERESA: She wants to feel that some peace has been made.

LOUISE: They went to supper at Palmer's—that's the really nice restaurant …

AGNES: (*to* THERESA) It's nothing to do with me …

LOUISE: She didn't even know she had a father.

THERESA: I know it's hard.

AGNES: It's not hard, it's not hard at all, because it's not going to happen.

LOUISE: He turned out to be really nice.

AGNES: Who?

LOUISE: Kara's father.

AGNES: I don't know any Kara.

LOUISE: Kara Ryan from *Ryan's Cove*.

THERESA: Let's just talk about it. Or just think about it.

AGNES: Talk about it all you like, think about it 'til your brain turns blue I don't care. "B" is right. But it's not "B" for Bradley. It's "B" for lousy, rotten, stinking bastard.

AGNES exits.

LOUISE: They had a really nice time. A nice dinner and all that. Then for about two weeks Kara got nice. Not making evil plans against her mother. Not running around on Justin. But the thing was she got kind of boring then. Until it turned out that her father was just trying to get money out of her to support his gambling addiction. Then she got bad and interesting again.

AGNES returns with her suitcase and some clothes in her arms.

THERESA: Where are you going?

AGNES: Look. I am a grown woman. I have my own life, I make my own decisions. I'm not going to be told who to see or when, I'm not going to be counting my drinks, I am not going to be instructed how to speak, or what to do, or when to do it. It's going to be better for everyone if I just go and stay in a hotel.

THERESA: Don't be silly.

AGNES: In a hotel where I can be as "silly" as I like.

THERESA: Always looking for an excuse.

AGNES: For what?

LOUISE: So you can drink without anybody knowing.

AGNES: I wasn't talking to you. Brat.

THERESA: To avoid whatever you find unpleasant.

AGNES: Don't talk to me about avoiding, Saint Theresa. You're the one who's avoiding. Out there in the bowels of New Brunswick, farming for God. Try living in the world for a week or two and then talk to me about avoiding things.

LOUISE: Agnes?

AGNES: No, I'm going. I refuse to stay here.

LOUISE: Then can I have my clicker back.

> *AGNES realizes she still has the remote control. She drops it on the table. LOUISE picks it up and exits. THERESA exits to her mother's bedroom. We hear the talk show again from the living room. AGNES stands in the room not sure what to do.*

AGNES: Fine then. Goodbye.

> *After a moment she exits. Light fades as the talk show continues.*

Scene 3

Later that night. THERESA sits at the table reading.
Some thumping off stage. After a few moments AGNES
enters with her suitcase. She is very tired and a little
drunk. AGNES plops herself down in a chair.

AGNES: What are you reading, Luke or John?

THERESA: Margaret Atwood.

AGNES: Where's the Mistress of the Air Waves?

THERESA: Asleep. It's two o'clock.

AGNES: Why aren't you in bed?

THERESA: I'm reading.

Silence.

AGNES: Why doesn't anything ever match up to our
imagining of it? Does Miss Margaret Atwood have an
answer for that one?

THERESA: I think for that you better try Luke.

AGNES: It was like Mother had that thing about Marion
Bridge. The way she used to talk about it as if it was
some kind of paradise. Everything was better there.
And every summer she'd get us all geared up about
going and then of course something or other would
come up—Dad would be off wherever, or one of us
would get sick, or Mother would be in a mood. And
then finally, finally, we end up going. I was … ten,
maybe twelve. And we were all beside ourselves about
the trip. You boiled eggs and we made sandwiches—
what was it fourteen miles or something? Guess we
didn't get out much back then. And on our way there
I remember we were being so good and quiet because
we didn't want anything to happen so that we

wouldn't get there. But we got to Marion Bridge and what was there? A few houses, a post office, a store, two churches and a dirt road leading down to the river. Just another town. And what did we do? We sat on the beach, we went for a walk and got chased by a dog who bit me, it started to rain, Mother and Dad fought and we went home early. I don't even think we ate our sandwiches. And that was the end of that. Here's me expecting paradise and it turned out to be just another rotten Sunday afternoon.

THERESA: Where have you been?

AGNES: Trying to find a hotel that would take my credit card.

THERESA: What kind is it?

AGNES: The over the limit kind.

Silence.

AGNES: I'm so old and I've got nothing.

THERESA: You've got your acting.

AGNES: My acting is turning out to be a very expensive, time-consuming and demoralizing hobby.

THERESA: You've got your friends.

AGNES: My friends are all alcoholics and drug addicts to whom I owe money.

THERESA: Oh well.

Silence.

AGNES: I'm just old and ugly.

THERESA: Don't forget mean.

AGNES: Thanks a lot.

THERESA: I'm mad at you.

AGNES: Look I'll see her tomorrow, I will, I swear.

THERESA: It's got nothing to do with me.

AGNES: Well well.

THERESA: I'm mad at you.

AGNES: I'm getting that drift, yeah.

THERESA: She's your mother Agnes, do you have any idea what that must feel like?

AGNES: Yes Theresa I do.

THERESA: Oh …

AGNES: Whatever.

THERESA: I didn't mean to …

AGNES: We talked about her tonight. I saw Sandy. He was at the bar with Charlie.

THERESA: And how's Sandy?

AGNES: Oh you know. Old. And sad.

THERESA: Fat and bald?

AGNES: He looks alright. A little plump. Not fat. Not yet anyway. I think he got hair implants but he's not talking. Charlie sort of hinted at it. He's not half bad really, Charlie. But God they're sloppy drunks. They're a good pair. One of them is crying while the other one's getting sick. They can keep it going for hours until they get confused and one of them is blubbering into the toilet and the other one is puking on your shoulder.

THERESA: You're bad.

Silence.

AGNES: We talked about her a little, Sandy and me. He
doesn't know too much—apparently she's not Joan
anymore. She's "Joanie" now. And they moved—all
the way up to Cape North. They've got a little craft
shop type thing. Sandy went up one day a year or so
ago. Sandy says she's got my eyes … Her name is
Joanie and she's got my eyes.

THERESA: You did the right thing.

AGNES: No I didn't. I didn't do anything. It wasn't up to
me was it. I wanted to keep her. But they shipped me
off to that bloody convent for six months to keep me
out of sight and then when she was born, that was
that, she was gone and I was supposed to forget about
the whole thing. And the worst of it was—and I don't
know if it was cruelty or stupidity—they let me hold
her before they took her away. They brought her in to
me for five minutes and I held her and I felt how
right that felt and nothing, nothing has ever felt that
right again. The next day Mother came to get me and
all the way home in the car all she talked about was
the goddamn weather. And that's why I can't go in
and see her Theresa—because she's in there dying
and because she's dying, I'd have to forgive her for
what she did. For letting it happen. And I can't
forgive her for that.

THERESA: You were so young.

AGNES: So what! So what! I was young but I knew what I
wanted. And that's more than I can say about myself
right now. I wanted to have a baby. That's what I
wanted. You say you had a calling, well I had one too.
I mean it's not like I knew that at the time. It's not
like I had any big scheme or anything. But when I
think about it now I must have known what I was
doing. What? You think I was in love with Sandy

Deveau? Come on! We had sex once! Once! That was a night, let me tell you. It took half a hit of acid and a bottle of vodka before he could even get it up.

THERESA: Agnes, too much information.

AGNES: I'll save it for my memoirs.

THERESA: You always were an unconventional girl.

AGNES: Surely wanting to have a child hasn't become unconventional.

THERESA: Well you could have had children. You could now, you could adopt or—

AGNES: I have a child! And sure yes I thought it would happen again—in some other situation—but it didn't. And I'd be nuts to bring a kid into my life now—I've screwed things up so bad the last thing I need is a kid in it. But she should have known. Mother should have known. And the thing is I think she did know. I wanted that baby and it was the right thing to do. But Mother and the bloody Church. No—I won't even blame the Church—because it was really just all about what would the neighbours think—all about bloody appearances. And I can't forgive her for that.

THERESA: You don't have to.

AGNES: Oh come on, that's what the whole thing is about, that's why I'm supposed to be here, that's how it works.

THERESA: Imagine it was you. You were up there and Joanie was you. People make mistakes. Don't they. You don't have to forgive her. You just have to love her, and let her love you.

AGNES sighs and starts to light a cigarette.

THERESA: Oh Agnes don't. Mother will smell it and be on and on about wanting one.

AGNES: She's up?

THERESA: Oh yes. She mostly sleeps through the afternoon. This is pretty much her best time really. She's not due for her pills for another hour. She's not as dopey as she gets.

> *Pause.*

THERESA: Why don't you go in? Just say hi.

AGNES: I don't know.

THERESA: I'll leave it to you. I'm going to see if I can catch a little sleep.

> *THERESA touches AGNES.*

THERESA: A very unconventional girl.

> *THERESA exits. AGNES sits alone. With resolve she stands and heads toward her mother's room. She stops. She returns to the table and picks up the flowers which still sit there. She moves toward her mother's room. She stops again. She returns to the table and picks up her cigarettes and matches. With flowers and cigarettes in hand she goes to see her mother.*

Scene 4

The next day. THERESA sits at the table. She looks through the many Post-it notes she has collected. We hear AGNES and LOUISE approaching the house.

LOUISE: (*off*) Of barbers: Saint Matthew. Of bee keepers: Saint Andrew. Of Bolivia: Our Lady of Capucdana. Of Boy Scouts: Saint George. Of brewers: Saint Luka. Of brides: Saint Nicholas. Of butchers: Saint Anthony the Abbot.

THERESA puts the notes back in her pocket. AGNES and LOUISE enter.

LOUISE: Of cab drivers: Saint Fiacre. Of Canada: Saint Anne and Saint Joseph. Of canoeists: Saint Raymond. Of childbirth: Saint Gerard Majella. Of cooks: Saint Martha. Of Cuba: Our Lady of Charity. Of dancers: Saint Vitus.

LOUISE passes through the room.

THERESA: Where were you two?

LOUISE: (*as she exits*) At the prayer group. Of dentists: Saint Apollonia. Of desperate situations: Saint Jude. Of doctors: Saint Luke. Of domestic animals: Saint Anthony.

THERESA: (*to AGNES*) And where were you?

AGNES: At the prayer group.

THERESA: What?

AGNES: Don't get your hopes up. I just wanted to check on what Louise was getting herself into.

THERESA: I see. And what's the verdict?

AGNES: I met Dory.

LOUISE re-enters.

LOUISE: Of Ecuador: The Sacred Heart. Of editors: Saint Clare. Of emigrants ... Of emigrants—Who the heck?

AGNES: She seemed very nice.

THERESA: Louise, what are you doing?

LOUISE: All the Patron Saints in alphabetical order of what they're patron of. Dory's teaching me—she knows every single one. I'm up to "e" but I can't remember "emigrants." Ecuador: Sacred Heart. Editors: Saint Clare. England: Saint George. But emigrants ...

LOUISE wanders off.

AGNES: So you must have met Dory then?

THERESA: Oh yes. At Mass and so on.

AGNES: She's interesting.

THERESA: She seems nice enough.

AGNES: Kind of a little ... butch ... don't you think?

THERESA: Kind of what?

AGNES: You know ... kind of ... strong.

THERESA: Well she runs that farm she's got all by herself.

AGNES: And the prayer meeting, that's quite something. People are awfully affectionate there. Lots of hugging and hand holding and so on.

THERESA: What do you mean by that?

AGNES: Nothing. It's nice.

THERESA: People get filled with the Spirit. They want to share their good feeling.

AGNES: "Filled with the Spirit." Mmm.

LOUISE re-enters.

LOUISE: Of emigrants is either Saint Patrick or Saint Francis Xavier Something.

AGNES: Well she certainly is quite a character.

LOUISE: Who is?

AGNES: Dory.

LOUISE: Dory's great. She don't take nothing from nobody. And you should see her truck. It's beautiful. But she's selling it though, because she wants to get a four-by-four.

AGNES: (*pointedly to THERESA*) A truck.

LOUISE: But she's selling it.

AGNES: Do you ever see Dory outside of the prayer group?

LOUISE: Mass.

AGNES: But outside of church I mean?

LOUISE: Like where?

AGNES: I don't know. Like a restaurant.

LOUISE: What restaurant?

AGNES: Any restaurant.

THERESA: Who's got money for that?

AGNES: Or have her over for dinner.

LOUISE: What do you mean?

AGNES: Some evening.

LOUISE: We don't have dinner in the evening.

AGNES: I mean supper. Or go to a movie or something.

LOUISE: What movie?

AGNES: Any movie—some movie you want to see.

LOUISE: Oh.

AGNES: It would be nice. Give her a call.

LOUISE: What do you mean?

AGNES: On the phone!

LOUISE: I don't have her number.

AGNES: Well you could get it.

LOUISE: Oh.

THERESA: Louise, go see if Mother touched her lunch at all.

AGNES: I'll go.

THERESA: Louise you go.

> LOUISE exits somewhat confused.

THERESA: What are you up to?

AGNES: I'm not up to anything. She doesn't have any friends. She should have some friends. She should get out more, you said that yourself.

THERESA: Look, I've got myself all worked up here.

AGNES: It's no big deal.

THERESA: Not about that. It's Mother—she's on and on about this—and look, I don't want to start anything here and please Agnes don't go getting all dramatic on me but—Mother keeps on about us going to see Dad.

AGNES: Well then maybe we should.

THERESA: What?

AGNES: Maybe we should.

THERESA: You've certainly changed your tune.

AGNES: I'm in a good mood today. I made a decision about something. I'm going to take a little drive. Up to Cape North.

THERESA: Oh Agnes …

AGNES: I just want to see her.

THERESA: Do you think that's such a good idea?

AGNES: They have a craft shop. I'm going shopping that's all. I want to get some … crafts.

THERESA: I don't think—

AGNES: I just want to see her. When I was sitting up there with Mother last night I realized … I mean we didn't say much. She wrote a couple of notes. And in a way the not talking was—it was like there was more truth in the silence or something. It was just the being there—there was something in it that was—it was a feeling—or more than that—a truth or—just a knowing—in a way that couldn't be denied. Whatever happened happened but she's my mother and I'm her daughter and that's just more—just realer than words or memories or anything else. Do you understand?

A beat. THERESA says nothing.

AGNES: I'm going to Cape North. I just want to see her.

THERESA: And you won't say a thing?

AGNES: Well, I'll say "hi" or "how are you" but I'm not going to say, "Hi, how are you I'm your mother."

THERESA: Oh Agnes …

AGNES: It's decided. Oh and look, I got this.

AGNES produces a small brass bell.

AGNES: For Mother when she needs something, just a little … (*She rings the bell.*)

THERESA: That's nice.

> *AGNES heads off toward her mother's room. She pauses.*

AGNES: And it's good that we should see Dad. I think it's a good idea.

> *AGNES exits. THERESA is alone.*

THERESA: Here we go.

Scene 5

Several days later. The stage is empty. A bell rings upstairs. LOUISE crosses through the room and out. She is wearing a skirt and her hair is wet. THERESA enters attacking her sweater with a lint brush. LOUISE re-enters.

LOUISE: Are we going or what?

THERESA: When Agnes gets back we'll go.

LOUISE: Well when's she getting back?

THERESA: When she gets here.

LOUISE: That's not an answer.

THERESA: Look at you!

LOUISE: What?

LOUISE plunks herself down in a chair.

THERESA: You're wearing a skirt!

LOUISE: So?

THERESA: You look nice in a skirt.

LOUISE: How come whenever I wear a skirt everybody goes "You're wearing a skirt!"?

THERESA: Well you hardly every wear a skirt.

LOUISE: 'Cause everybody's always talking about it when I do.

THERESA: It's nice you're wearing a skirt.

LOUISE: If we ever get to go.

THERESA: Aren't you missing your show?

LOUISE: Which one?

THERESA: Ryan's Thingy.

LOUISE: *Ryan's Cove*. Ah it's getting so dumb. Nothing ever happens on it.

THERESA: Seems to me like lots happens on it.

LOUISE: But nothing ever ends up anywhere. It's so not realistic. Like the identical cousin thing. Or that time Kara was a werewolf but Justin just ended up dreaming it. A two-week dream! Come on! And now they've got aliens landing in the cove.

> *The bell rings upstairs.*

LOUISE: I'll go. I've gotta do something, I'm going nuts waiting. Should I put on pants?

THERESA: No. You look nice.

> *The bell rings upstairs. LOUISE exits. THERESA is alone. After a moment she goes into the living room. She turns on the television. She flips through channels searching for something, finally we hear the following dialogue.*

JUSTIN: "But Kara don't you understand he's an alien."

KARA: "Don't be silly Justin, no alien could make love to a woman like he does."

JUSTIN: "What! Kara! What are you saying?"

KARA: "I'm saying … read my lips Justin … I'm saying I feel like a woman for the first time in my life."

> *AGNES enters in a state. She circles the room once and then exits. THERESA turns off the television and re-enters. AGNES re-enters with a drink.*

THERESA: You're back.

> *AGNES drinks it down in one shot.*

THERESA: Well what happened?

AGNES exits. After a moment she returns with another drink.

THERESA: Agnes …

AGNES: It's alright it's my first of the day.

THERESA: Second.

AGNES: That was my first.

She downs the shot.

AGNES: That was my second.

THERESA: What happened?

AGNES: I saw her.

THERESA: You saw her.

AGNES: I saw her. I talked to her.

THERESA: You told her?

AGNES: No. But I talked to her.

THERESA: What was she like?

During the following speech AGNES exits and returns with another drink which she sips throughout.

AGNES: She's beautiful. She's just … She's built sort of like Louise and she's got your face and my hair—but Mother's eyes, not mine at all. And thank God I think she got off lucky because I couldn't see a trace of Sandy in her.

THERESA: What happened?

AGNES: Well I went into the store. Her and her … God I find it hard to say … Her and her mother have this craft store. It's nice, you know, simple. She's trying to get her high school to—she never got her high school—because she wants to go to teacher's college.

She wants to be a teacher! Isn't that a good job—
that's a job that makes a difference. But she's waiting
until her boyfriend—oh my God she's got a
boyfriend—she's waiting til her boyfriend—Steve I
think—finishes technical school somewhere for
mechanics or ... I think she said maintenance. Which,
what is maintenance, do people go to technical
school to be a janitor—because I don't know, with her
a teacher they seem like maybe they're on different
paths don't you think? But she hates Cape North and
she loves *Jane Eyre.*

THERESA: Jane Eyre?

AGNES: She's reading it for her English. And she loves to
laugh, but she hates Cape North and she's desperate
to get out.

THERESA: How did you find all this out?

AGNES: I talked to her! She was just desperate to talk to
somebody ... I met the mother.

THERESA: You did?

AGNES: I don't like her. Cold. Not at all friendly. Nothing
like Joanie. Joanie. Oh my God.

THERESA: What do you mean cold?

AGNES: Nothing like Joanie. Cold. Just cold. They don't
get along, you can tell.

THERESA: Agnes.

AGNES: What? Nothing! I'm just saying what I saw.

THERESA: What are you thinking?

AGNES: I'm not thinking anything. Anyway we'll see what
happens Wednesday.

THERESA: What's Wednesday?

AGNES: My pottery class.

THERESA: Pottery class?

AGNES: The mother ... Chrissy, she teaches a pottery class at the store a few times a week and Joanie helps out with it.

THERESA: Agnes.

AGNES: We'll just get to be friendly that's all. And from what I can tell she sure needs a friend.

THERESA: It's not a good idea.

AGNES: It's fine. It's nothing. And I always liked pottery.

THERESA: Since when?

AGNES: Since lately.

> *LOUISE enters.*

LOUISE: It's about time! Let's go.

AGNES: Go where?

THERESA: We're having dinner at Dad's.

AGNES: Oh no, I totally forgot.

LOUISE: What do you mean?

THERESA: Are you alright for it? Do you want to postpone it?

LOUISE: Noooo!

AGNES: No, fine, no, let's get it all done in a day that's the way to do it. What time did we say we'd be there?

LOUISE: Long ago!

THERESA: Now.

AGNES: Alright. Good. Here's the deal: we are going to go out as a happy united little family to our father's house and have dinner with him and his ... little Lolita.

LOUISE: Connie.

AGNES: Whatever. We will eat our meal, I will not drink two bottles of wine and attack him with a butter knife, exactly ninety minutes after we arrive we will leave, and then we will come home and tell Mother we had a wonderful time and that will be the end of it.

LOUISE: What if we do have a wonderful time?

AGNES: Then we'd have to bring an umbrella, what with all the pigs flying.

LOUISE: Huh?

AGNES: Maybe it'll be lovely.

THERESA: I'm just not sure about leaving Mother.

AGNES: We'll be back in two hours. Did she take her pills?

LOUISE: I just gave them to her.

THERESA: I don't know. I could always stay and—

AGNES: Mother wants us all to go, that's part of the deal.

THERESA: It's not so much him I mind seeing as Lolita.

LOUISE: Connie.

THERESA: Whatever.

AGNES: So while I'm at him with the butter knife you can get her with the fork.

LOUISE: Are we going or what?

AGNES: (*finishing her drink*) Come on troops! To the front line!

THERESA: Alright.

AGNES: Oh my!

LOUISE: What?

AGNES: You're wearing a skirt!

LOUISE: I'm changing!

AGNES: No you look great, come on.

> *The three women start out. They talk as they exit.*

AGNES: Oh what's up with the aliens?

LOUISE: I don't know, that show's getting so dumb.

AGNES: I like that blond alien guy.

THERESA: Apparently so does Kara.

AGNES: How do you know?

THERESA: Oh, I just caught a bit of it looking for the news.

Scene 6

Later that evening THERESA, AGNES and LOUISE enter.

THERESA: I can't believe it! I just can't believe it! It's scandalous! It's criminal! It's just … And the way she went on! The queen of the castle! And did you look at him!

LOUISE: That was so no fun.

THERESA: So no fun! No fun indeed! Infuriating more like it!

LOUISE: I'll go see Mother.

LOUISE exits.

THERESA: I almost had a drink I swear. I was that angry.

AGNES: Don't get yourself in a state.

AGNES exits.

THERESA: Get?! Get?! I'm gone! I'm there! And it's not a state either it's bigger. It's a province. No, bigger! It's a country! It's a continent!

AGNES returns with two shots. She offers one to THERESA.

THERESA: Don't be ridiculous.

AGNES pours THERESA's shot into her glass.

AGNES: At least it's over with.

THERESA: I'm beside myself! On both sides. This one here and this one here and they're both angrier than I am! I can't believe how you can be so calm.

AGNES: You're worked up enough for all of us. Anyway she's just another one of those Deena Jessome types.

THERESA: Who?

AGNES: You know Deena Jessome. From school. Dougie's sister.

THERESA: Oh yes well she was … yes, but she was …

AGNES: A slut.

THERESA: Agnes.

AGNES: She was. She went out with the whole hockey team.

THERESA: Well she had a lot of dates.

AGNES: The whole hockey team at the same time.

THERESA: But I liked Deena Jessome. At least she was what she was and was honest about it. Not like little Lolita. Oh dear! I've got to … I don't know what I've got to do. I should have a cup of tea. No that'll just wind me up more. Perhaps I should just head to bed. But there's not much chance of me sleeping bolt upright and raving is there.

AGNES: It wasn't so bad.

THERESA: It wasn't so bad? Her acting the happy little housewife. She didn't even know how to operate the stove! What does she feed him? You couldn't even eat the turkey, it was that tough. And I don't know who would have the nerve to call those grey things potatoes. And what was she wearing?

AGNES: A halter top.

THERESA: A little piece of nothing and some string. And prancing around like some kind of … And that house! Who needs five bedrooms? And that awful little dog. "Baby"! What kind of name is that for a dog? And Dad never liked dogs. And she's getting two more, did you hear her when she said she was getting two more? And a dishwasher! She can't use the stove what's she going to do with a dishwasher? Unless she's going to use it to wash the dogs.

AGNES: I feel sorry for her.

THERESA: Sorry for her? And who was the fella in the basement!?

AGNES: Her cousin she said.

THERESA: Her cousin? I'm sure!

AGNES: Well well what are you thinking—perhaps you've been spending a bit too much time with *Ryan's Cove.*

THERESA: Come on! What's she got her cousin there for?

AGNES: You heard her, he's just there to help build the pool.

THERESA: The pool! The pool! What in the name of all that is good and holy does Dad need with a pool? He can't even make it up and down the stairs by himself.

AGNES: Well it was his choice to be with her.

THERESA: And her calling him "Daddy." If that's not enough to turn you off your meal.

AGNES: Well you found the turkey tough anyway.

THERESA: And what a mess he's in.

AGNES: (*laughing*) "Pass the binoculars."

THERESA: What?

AGNES: "Pass the binoculars."

THERESA: Oh no I know.

AGNES: (*laughing*) "Pass the binoculars."

THERESA: Oh I know, don't laugh.

AGNES: But you've got to hand it to her though, cool as a cucumber. He says "Pass the binoculars," and she just passes him a roll like nothing's wrong.

THERESA: She made a joke of it.

AGNES: Well what else are you going to do?

THERESA: And he couldn't even remember Louise's name.

AGNES: It can't be much of a life for her though.

THERESA: Oh come on, she's got poor old Dad's pension and the mansion on the hill and the cousin in the basement.

AGNES: And when the phone rang and he says, "Get the tub."

THERESA: (*laughing*) Oh no, I know, don't laugh.

AGNES: But he was pretty close though with the rolls. I mean they were hard as binoculars.

THERESA: (*laughing*) Stop.

AGNES: (*laughing*) "Pass the binoculars and get the tub."

THERESA: (*laughing*) The binoculars were so tough they should have had a good soak in the phone before she served them!

AGNES: Poor Connie.

THERESA: Serves her right.

    LOUISE enters.

AGNES: How's Mother? Louise? How's Mother?

THERESA: Louise? How's Mother?

LOUISE: She wouldn't wake up. I tried but she wouldn't.

THERESA: Oh good Lord …

THERESA exits to Mother's room. AGNES rises to exit.

LOUISE: I tried to wake her up but she wouldn't. And I leaned down and I said to her, "Mother?" I said. And I was going to tell her about being at Dad's but I was going to make it sound nice and that. And I said "Mother?" But she wouldn't wake up. So I touched her arm. I touched her arm and I could tell that she wasn't there. She was there but she wasn't there. Part of her was there but the part of her that was there wasn't her. She's up there but she's not. Where is she?

THERESA re-enters, upset.

THERESA: Agnes. She's gone.

AGNES: Oh God. Oh God.

THERESA: She was all alone.

AGNES: She was all alone.

LOUISE: She had this in her hand.

LOUISE holds up a note.

THERESA: She was all alone.

The women do not touch. They remain separate as the light fades.

LOUISE: It's a heart.

AGNES: She was alone.

LOUISE: A little heart.

ACT TWO

Scene 1

We hear a young girl singing the hymn "Be Not Afraid" in a strong, clear voice. Light up on THERESA. She addresses the audience.

THERESA: On the farm where I live we have animals—two cows and some chickens, a rooster, a tired old horse called Matilda and more cats than we can keep track of. And from the animals we get milk, and eggs, and lots of kittens. Now we've got a tractor but when I first got there about ten years ago we used Matilda to haul the tiller—the Sisters there believe that it's best to use living things to make living things. From the earth, for the earth. And some of them say that the vegetables were better—bigger and tastier—when Matilda did the work, but most of them have come around to seeing a tractor as a kind of a living thing: you've got to clean it and you've got to feed it and it has a real temperament. Farming is wonderful: getting your hands down there in the beautiful dirt. When you're working in it up to your elbows it starts to feel like liquid, thick dark liquid, like the blood of the earth. And that's really all I've got: the farm, the animals, the earth. And my faith. But lately I've been wondering if I'm there more for the farm than the faith. But one thing about the faith I know is right is the idea of owning nothing, having nothing but each day. Although since I've been back home … I've never been one for collecting anything but there's something about these …

She takes a large collection of the Post-it notes from her pocket.

THERESA: Mother's notes. They're so beautiful. At first just a bunch of marks and squiggles but once you understand it it's as big and wonderful as any language. I let on they were for Louise but really they're my special connection to Mother. We always got on, me and Mother, but in that way that there's not too much to say. With Agnes there was turmoil and tumult and Louise always had her odd ways, but I was the one in the middle. The good one, the peace-maker. There was never too much need for drama between Mother and me. There was her drinking— but I wasn't really supposed to know about that—and I guess I chose not to know. And once Dad left well it didn't seem like she had much more than her few drinks every night and her books. She always had a book on the go. But the funny thing is … I remember one day when I was little she was reading a book and she had that sort of dreamy look on her face that she got when she read and I watched her—she didn't know I was there but I watched her for a long time, maybe as long as fifteen minutes—and in all that time she never turned a page and I realized that she just used the book as a kind of a decoy. A trick she used to escape into her own world. Wherever that was. And I guess the distance between Mother and her secret world is the same distance I've put between the world and me. But all these, these little notes, this language, these make me feel like I'm part of … that I understand something.

It was a lovely service. Father Dave spoke beautifully. Mother's favourite hymns. Agnes read from John. Mother loved John and Agnes was always so good to read. It didn't take us long to realize that Mother had arranged for the circumstances of her departure. She wanted to be alone. It was her final choice. No resolution. She left this world as she wished to, on her own. In her secret world. And there's a certain beauty in that I suppose. And a strangeness too. But people are strange. Never what you expect. Not like the farm. From the soil you can expect the vegetables and from the animals you can expect the milk and the eggs and the kittens. But from people … Best not to have expectations and to keep your plans flexible.

> *THERESA gathers up the notes.*

THERESA: Today I went to look at the stone. It's lovely. Praying hands on one side and an open book on the other. I find it particularly fitting that the book is marble. The pages will never turn.

> *The light shifts. THERESA turns and watches as AGNES enters and takes off her coat. AGNES paces back and forth.*

THERESA: What are you all wound up about?

AGNES: Nothing nothing.

THERESA: Are you sure?

AGNES: Yes, no, nothing.

THERESA: You know Louise still hasn't come out of her room today. Dory called again but she wouldn't even take the phone. Might be partly to do with Mother's insurance cheque coming. Got her down all over again. I told her maybe we could use it toward a new car. I thought that might cheer her up but no doing. Might be nice if you spent some time with Louise. What's the matter? How was your pottery class?

AGNES: Oh dear.

THERESA: What is it?

AGNES: She's a monster Theresa.

THERESA: Who is?

AGNES: The mother. Chrissy. She's awful with her.

THERESA: How?

AGNES: See the story is—which I just got—see after Chrissy got Joanie her husband took off and she got together with this other guy and they ended up having two of their own and well I guess the sun just shines right out of their … you know. And Joanie she just can't do a thing right.

THERESA: Where are you getting this?

AGNES: From Joanie.

THERESA: Well she's young, you know she's going to say—

AGNES: I've seen it! I've got eyes. I see how she treats her. She's not good with her. And she's wild Joanie is. The boyfriend Steve is home from his technical school and she dropped her summer course and apparently she's in the bar every night with him—and I don't like the look of him. Trouble in a cap Steve is. See she has no proper guidance.

THERESA: Agnes.

AGNES: What?

THERESA: Where's this headed?

AGNES: Nowhere. I don't know. Nowhere. She needs help.

THERESA: She's not a child.

AGNES: No but she is in a way. She's had no guidance.

THERESA: You're probably not getting the whole story.

AGNES: I can feel it Theresa. In my gut. It's a troubled situation.

THERESA: Yes well we've got situations here.

AGNES: She's my daughter.

THERESA: But she doesn't know that.

AGNES: But if she did—

THERESA: Agnes. Look. I understand your concern and so on but don't you think you should spend a little time with Louise? She's going through something here.

AGNES: Well we're all going through something.

THERESA: Yes but you've lost people before, I've lost people, Louise hasn't. I try to talk to her but she doesn't hear me.

AGNES: I've spent time with her.

THERESA: How many times have you been to Cape North since the funeral?

AGNES: Four or five.

THERESA: Six. You have barely spent a proper day here and when you are here all you're thinking about is … well, whatever scheme it is you're hatching.

AGNES: I'm not hatching anything.

THERESA: Ha!

AGNES rises and moves to exit.

AGNES: Get off my back.

THERESA: Yes that's it, go have a few drinks that'll sort things out fine.

AGNES: What?

THERESA: Go on, just like always.

AGNES: Listen sister darling, I haven't had a drink since the funeral. What you've got here is the real me, one hundred percent full out Agnes MacKeigan, unbuzzed and unsedated. The creature in nature as it was born, all for your viewing and listening pleasure. But if you're trying to drive me to it you're doing a hell of a job.

THERESA: You're still drunk though. Maybe not with booze but now it's with that girl. You just traded one for the other. All your thoughts with her when they should be with your family.

AGNES: Joanie is my family.

THERESA: We're your family. Louise is your family. And it's not just Mother either. That Dory's calling here three or four times a day. Something's going on and there's no denying you've had a hand in it.

AGNES: What the hell do you mean by that?

THERESA: I mean what I mean.

AGNES: Which is what?

THERESA: "Why don't you have her for supper? Rent a movie." The sly little grin—all smart and worldly.

AGNES: There's no harm in her having a friend. I didn't know she'd become cloistered.

THERESA: I wasn't born yesterday. I hear what people say about Dory Ferguson.

AGNES: Which is what?

THERESA: Which is … whatever.

AGNES: Say it. What?

LOUISE appears suddenly.

THERESA: Well if it isn't sleeping beauty.

LOUISE: I wasn't sleeping. What are you talking about?

THERESA: Oh you know.

AGNES: Nothing.

LOUISE: Nothing?

AGNES: No nothing.

LOUISE: Your mouths were moving and words were coming out but you were talking about nothing?

AGNES: Nothing really.

LOUISE: Nothing really for me to know. Just like everything.

THERESA: What everything?

LOUISE: Everything everything. Like when Dad left and everybody said he was on a trip. Like Mother not even saying goodbye. Like everything. Like Marion Bridge that time.

THERESA: What time.

LOUISE: That time you all went to Marion Bridge and I didn't.

AGNES: We only went the one time. You were there.

LOUISE: Was not. It was supposed to be all special and that and then I had the chicken pox and Mother said we'd wait 'til next week but Dad said no you were going anyway and you two made egg salad sandwiches and went off without me.

AGNES: You weren't there?

LOUISE: That's what I'm saying and I had to stay here with Deena Jessome babysitting me with all them boys around who I hated and then you all came back and you gave me the egg salad sandwiches to make me feel better but I couldn't eat them because they were all sat on, and I was sick right, I couldn't eat them anyway even if they weren't sat on, and I ended up getting sicker on top of the chicken pox because Deena Jessome's boyfriends kept me locked out of the house all afternoon and it rained.

AGNES: Where's this coming from?

LOUISE: I never get to be part of nothing.

AGNES: We can go to Marion Bridge. We can go tomorrow.

LOUISE: No! No it's too late. Dad's gone and Mother's gone and I never get to be part of anything. Always always 'cause I'm strange or something. (*to AGNES*) And you're gone all the time. Where do you go all the time?

AGNES: Nowhere.

LOUISE: Lie! Tell me.

AGNES: Nowhere.

LOUISE: Nowhere's nowhere. Where's nowhere? Tell me.

AGNES: No.

LOUISE: See! See!

LOUISE exits.

AGNES: Christ.

THERESA: See?

AGNES: Get. Off. My. Back.

THERESA: Finish cleaning your own house before you
start on the neighbours.

AGNES: That would be Luke would it? Or Corinthians?

THERESA: Such a comedian.

THERESA picks up the car keys and moves to exit.

AGNES: Where are you going?

THERESA: Nowhere.

She moves to exit and then stops.

THERESA: Will you be here when I get back?

AGNES: Not if you're lucky.

THERESA: So be it.

*THERESA exits. AGNES paces back and forth in the
kitchen. She goes to exit. She stops. She sits. She rises
and moves to exit. She stops. She plunks herself down in
the chair. She growls in frustration. She drops her head
to her chest. She sits up. After a moment:*

AGNES: Louise!!

Scene 2

Later that evening. AGNES and LOUISE sit at the table playing cards.

AGNES: (*placing a card on the pile*) Oh I hate to do it but I've got nothing but that.

LOUISE moves to draw from the deck.

AGNES: Aren't you going for hearts?

LOUISE: Yeah.

AGNES: Well I just threw out the Queen.

LOUISE: Oh yeah.

LOUISE picks up AGNES's discard.

LOUISE: Rummy.

AGNES: Oh you won again!

LOUISE: (*unenthusiastically*) Hooray.

AGNES: Another hand?

LOUISE: I don't care.

AGNES: Your deal.

LOUISE: Go ahead.

AGNES shuffles and deals. They play throughout.

AGNES: So how are you?

LOUISE: How come you keep asking me that?

AGNES: Because you haven't answered.

LOUISE: Fine.

AGNES: What are you thinking about?

LOUISE: I don't know.

AGNES: Mother?

LOUISE: I guess.

AGNES: What about her?

LOUISE: I don't know.

Silence.

LOUISE: Do you think … Do you think she's in heaven?

AGNES: Of course she is.

LOUISE: Stuart from the prayer group says you have to spend until the end of time in limbo even if you were really really good and then when the world ends pretty much only saints get into heaven.

AGNES: Yes but it's different for mothers.

LOUISE: Is it?

AGNES: Oh yeah.

LOUISE: Oh. So she's in heaven.

AGNES: Playing cards with Saint Peter.

LOUISE: She liked Saint Jude.

AGNES: They're playing bridge and Saint Jude is her partner.

LOUISE: And what about us.

AGNES: What about us?

LOUISE: Will we go to heaven?

AGNES: Well by that time Mother will be in with all of the big shots up there and she'll have some pull so I don't see why not.

Silence.

LOUISE: How old is she, like in heaven?

AGNES: What do you mean?

LOUISE: Well is she like old as she was when she died and kind of sick and that?

AGNES: In heaven you get to choose whatever age you want to be.

LOUISE: Really?

AGNES: Uh huh.

LOUISE: So she could choose like eleven or eighteen or six or something?

AGNES: Whatever she wanted to be.

LOUISE: So say she chose eleven.

AGNES: Uh huh.

LOUISE: So if she chose eleven or six or something or some age she was before we knew her how would we recognize her when we got there?

AGNES: Well …

LOUISE: Maybe what we could do is go through all the pictures of her that we've got and put them all in order of how old she was and then we'd remember what she looked like from when she was a baby.

AGNES: I think that's an excellent idea.

LOUISE: Your go.

AGNES: Sorry?

LOUISE: I threw you go.

AGNES: Oh right.

> AGNES *picks a card. They continue to play. Silence.*

AGNES: And so how else are you?

LOUISE: What do you mean?

AGNES: I mean is there anything else on your mind?

LOUISE: I don't know. Like what?

AGNES: Like I don't know. Like something you're feeling?

LOUISE: Feeling how?

AGNES: Just feeling. Or thinking about.

LOUISE: I don't know.

AGNES: Because sometimes it helps to talk about things.

LOUISE: You talk.

AGNES: I am talking.

LOUISE: No you're not, you're asking questions.

    Silence.

LOUISE: It's your go.

AGNES: Louise? What's bothering you? I mean really.

LOUISE: I don't know. Nothing. Or I don't know.
Something, I guess. It's your go.

AGNES: I think I might know what it is.

LOUISE: Yeah?

AGNES: I think so.

LOUISE: It's your go.

    AGNES continues to play.

AGNES: Like something about someone?

LOUISE: I don't know.

AGNES: Like something about Dory?

LOUISE: I don't know. Yeah.

AGNES: Look honey, nobody can tell you the right thing to think or the right thing to do but you know inside what's right. If you feel something or want something then that's okay—and you can talk about anything you want to talk about with me.

Silence.

AGNES: Or if it's something to do with Dory then you can talk to her about it. But you shouldn't keep things inside you should talk about them. And I just want you to know—Louise listen to me—I just want you to know that whatever you feel it's okay. Nobody can tell you what's right for you.

LOUISE: Yeah?

AGNES: Yeah. You do what you need to do.

LOUISE: Okay.

AGNES: Are you okay?

LOUISE: Yeah. Are you okay?

AGNES: Of course I'm okay.

AGNES rises and gives LOUISE a hug.

LOUISE: Yikes! What's this for?

AGNES: Because I love you.

LOUISE: Get out of here. It's your go.

AGNES sits and discards. LOUISE picks it up.

LOUISE: Rummy.

AGNES: How did you do that?

LOUISE shuffles the cards.

LOUISE: You should talk less and watch your cards more.

Scene 3

A week later. The stage is empty. We hear Ryan's Cove *dialogue in the living room.*

KARA: "Oh Justin I'm sorry. I didn't mean to hurt you.

JUSTIN: "I know you didn't my love I know."

THERESA backs onto the stage from the living room. She is holding the remote control, mesmerized by the television.

KARA: "You know what I'd like to do my darling?"

JUSTIN: "What sweet one?"

KARA: "Let's go for a lovely drive in the country."

THERESA: No no don't do it! It's a trick!

JUSTIN: "That would be wonderful."

THERESA: No no she's in with the aliens! Don't do it!

KARA: "Yes absolutely wonderful."

THERESA: That Kara she's just pure evil.

AGNES enters. THERESA turns off the television and sticks the remote in her pocket.

THERESA: Hello.

AGNES: Yes. Hi. Where's Louise?

THERESA: Out to the prayer group.

AGNES: That's good. She seems better doesn't she?

THERESA: Yes. It's good you've been spending some time with her.

AGNES: Yes.

THERESA: And managing to keep up your pottery classes at the same time.

AGNES: Mmm.

THERESA: And how's that going?

AGNES: Well you know I'm not really too much for getting my hands dirty and it's hard to do that pottery stuff without making quite a mess. You know. Um.

THERESA: Something on your mind?

AGNES: Oh nothing.

THERESA: Nothing is it?

AGNES: Oh no not really too much not really no.

THERESA: I see. (*She heads to exit.*) Well I'm just going to go for a—

AGNES: Well no, well actually …

THERESA: Actually?

AGNES: Actually. (*She clears her throat.*) I had a lovely day.

THERESA: Did you?

AGNES: Yes. I uh … I skipped class today and Joanie and I spent the afternoon together.

THERESA: Did you? That's nice I guess.

AGNES: Yes it was. And um …

THERESA: Mm hm?

AGNES: Well.

THERESA: Well?

AGNES: There's a little … thing.

THERESA: A thing.

AGNES: Uh huh.

THERESA: What kind of thing?

AGNES: A thing. A sort of a wrinkle.

THERESA: A wrinkle.

AGNES: An interesting development.

THERESA: Interesting?

AGNES: I guess you could call it I suppose if you wanted to a bit of a problem.

THERESA: A problem.

AGNES: But perhaps if you wanted to you might see it not so much as a problem as an opportunity.

THERESA: Agnes do you think we might cut to the chase here?

AGNES: (*She clears her throat.*) It seems that things have reached a head between Joanie and the mother.

THERESA: Chrissy.

AGNES: Chrissy yes.

THERESA: Um hm.

AGNES: They had words and Chrissy put her out of the house and Joanie has nowhere to stay—the last couple of days she's been staying with a girl she knows—this tiny tiny little place, barely room for one really, not even a proper kitchen.

THERESA: Agnes?

AGNES: And I just thought that it might be a good idea that she come and stay here for a while.

THERESA: With us?

AGNES: Well you'll be leaving soon anyway.

THERESA: I'm in no rush, they said I could take the time I need. And frankly I could use a bit of time.

AGNES: Well that's fine, there's lots of room for all of us.

THERESA: And what about you? I thought you were going home soon. That's what you call Toronto now isn't it, home?

AGNES: I can always go back.

THERESA: Did you tell her?

AGNES: What?

THERESA: Who you were?

AGNES: No no. Not yet. Maybe later. When things settle down a bit.

THERESA: I just don't think it's a very good idea.

AGNES: Why not?

THERESA: We could—Maybe we could scrape up a bit of money to help her out but I don't think moving in here is the answer.

AGNES: Why not?

THERESA: And she's not a child. She can get a job—get her own place.

AGNES: She's family.

THERESA: You're doing it again Agnes.

AGNES: Look, this is a chance for me—This is an opportunity for me to set some things right. Mistakes were made in the past—and I'm not blaming anyone anymore, there's no point in that. I'm just saying that this is a chance to make something good happen.

THERESA: No.

AGNES: Why not?

THERESA: No.

AGNES: Don't say no, say maybe.

THERESA: No.

AGNES: I just need you to say that you think it might be a good idea. And now that you're going to be here well you'll be part of it too.

THERESA: No Agnes.

AGNES: Why not?

THERESA: Agnes, we've got Louise up to who knows what and you're an excuse away from a two day binge and I'm spending more time with Justin and Kara than in church.

AGNES: I haven't had a drink in almost a month!

THERESA: Yes and how many times have you done that before and how many times have you gone back?

AGNES: Thanks for your support.

THERESA: No … Look … You said yourself your life was too messed up to think about having a child in it.

AGNES: Yes, my life as it was! But now it's changing!

THERESA: Oh yes.

AGNES: You don't think I can change?

THERESA: Like the weather.

AGNES: Look, she wouldn't be in my life as my child, she just thinks she's my friend you see, so there wouldn't be any of those sort of complications. See?

THERESA: I thought she was family.

AGNES: Family to us, friend to her.

THERESA: Agnes, get your story straight.

AGNES: That's what I'm trying to do. I'm trying to get my story straight. I've spent so long trying to tell other people's stories. Telling stories in dirty basements with people who think crazy means brilliant and brilliant means poor. Telling stories I don't even understand. I want my story. And I made a mess of it—I let other people make a mess of it, now I can fix it.

THERESA: Dear we've none of us got a clue where we're headed—

AGNES: It could be great. We'll all figure things out together.

THERESA: Yes, a perfect fairy tale.

AGNES: It's the right thing to do.

THERESA: You don't even know this girl.

AGNES: I do.

THERESA: And how would you explain her to Louise?

AGNES: Louise knows a lot more than you think.

THERESA: No.

AGNES: Mother would want it.

THERESA: Oh come on.

AGNES: She would. If she were upstairs right now I'd go up and tell her and she'd get out her notes and draw a little heart.

THERESA: No.

AGNES: It'll be great.

THERESA: I'm saying no. Not here. Not now.

AGNES: Yes.

THERESA: For once in your life would you stop thinking of yourself Agnes?

AGNES: It is her I'm thinking of. She's got no one. She's scared. Chrissy she won't have anything to do with her and Steve the boyfriend well he's turned out to be the ass I expected—Theresa she's got no one.

THERESA: Oh stop it. That poor girl has nothing to do with it, you're only concerned about yourself.

AGNES: How can you say that?

THERESA: Because I know you.

AGNES: You think you always know everything, you think you've got it all worked out. Holy Saint Theresa all giving and kind but really you just don't want anyone else to have a life. Not me not Louise. You don't want anyone else to have a life because you don't have one. That's why you're such a bitch.

THERESA: Oh that's lovely.

AGNES: Well. You are.

THERESA: You have no idea about me Agnes, you just have no idea. You think it's all so easy for me but it's not, it's not. This is a life I have, a big life. I'd like to see you try being a nun. People say awful things—they think worse things. And I have a heart you know, I didn't give my heart up when I took my vows. And yes indeed I do live in the world. In this big old awful sick mess of a world. And my heart is filled with questions. Filled. Every time I look around at the world. And when I do look at it what I see is—No, what I don't see is God. You've got children killing children and half the world on drugs and the other half starving and people just letting it happen. Where's God in that? And I'm supposed to believe God is everywhere, in everything, in everyone—but sometimes I just don't see God. Imagine how that makes me feel—just as a person—as a person who made a decision and a promise to believe—to see God everywhere. But where is God? Every day—every minute of every day I have to ask that question because of the choices I've made. And you don't think sometimes I don't just feel like a fool? But I've got to keep believing and I've got to keep loving and giving and helping. But it's all such a mess and I don't know what to do about it. I don't know how to make things right. I don't know how I got here. There's no room Agnes … I have no room for anyone else …

AGNES comforts THERESA.

Scene 4

LOUISE addresses the audience.

LOUISE: On the highway and driving, the radio on a
really good song. I won't say what the song is 'cause
you say one song and somebody hates that song—
some people like country and some people like heavy
rock some people like no singing, so just say the song
is your favourite song. Favourite song, on the highway,
driving. Nothing ahead of you, nothing in your
rearview mirror. And the day say, say it's the day.
Daytime driving is one thing, night-time driving that's
something else. Night-time driving, that's heading
into yourself but daytime driving is heading out into
the world, and here we're talking about heading out
out out into the whole world. So it's daytime,
summertime, say about six o'clock, and say you're
heading east so that the sun's right behind you—and
everything all around you is that kind of orange kind
of yellow kind of golden kind of colour. And you're in
your machine—your car, or your truck or your
hatchback or whatever it is you've got—and there's a
warm wind, the window down, and what you got
around you is trees and fields and hills and stuff, and
what you got ahead of you is a long long line of road,
and what you got under you is this machine. Then
there's one thing you shouldn't be doing and one
thing you should be. The thing you shouldn't be
doing is to have a picture in your head of where
you're going, people do that—the whole time they're
driving they're just imagining the place they're going
so that they're not really driving they're really just
trying to get somewhere. So you shouldn't have a
place in your head. Maybe you shouldn't even know
where you're going, you'll only know where it is when

you get there. That would be best. And the thing you should be doing is staying really really still. Say you got your arm out the window like this and your hand on the wheel like this and your eyes on the road with your head like this. And you just stay like that, really really still. Of course you're steering a little bit right, just a little bit, just like this. And after a while if you're not thinking about getting somewhere and you're being really really still, then it's not like you're steering the machine on the road, it's like the road is steering the machine, and then it's like you're steering the road, and then it's like the road is coming in through the front of the machine and moving right through your body and shooting out the back, it's like the fields and the trees and the hills are these green lines in the golden light all around you and you are the machine you're in and you are the road under you, and you are the wind and the air and the light and the music and the empty mirror, and it is all moving so quickly and at the same time staying so still … moving, still, moving, still, both exactly perfectly, moving, still, both at the same time, and everything is you and you are everything.

You might think that'd be strange to think that way but that's okay because people think I'm strange anyway. And maybe I am some ways. I was thinking it might be 'cause I was the only one of the three of us not named for a saint. There's no Saint Louise. And I know 'cause I've been through them all. I haven't got them memorized yet but I'm working on it. But for sure there's no Saint Louise. Maybe there could be someday though. Saint Louise of the Highway. Strange. But see for me it's like everybody's strange, it's just that some people show it more than other people do. I suppose some people would say it's

strange for me to be standing here talking to you.
And I suppose some people'd say it's strange for you
to be sitting there listening.

Scene 5

A week later. AGNES is on her hands and knees scrubbing the floor. LOUISE enters.

LOUISE: What are you doing?

AGNES: I'm writing a biography of Winston Churchill.

LOUISE: What?

AGNES: Louise, what does it look like I'm doing?

LOUISE: Like you're scrubbing the floor?

AGNES: Brava.

LOUISE: What?

AGNES: Yes. I am scrubbing the floor.

LOUISE: But didn't you do that yesterday?

AGNES: I missed a spot.

LOUISE: Oh. You okay?

AGNES: Wonderful. Are you going somewhere?

LOUISE: Yeah I'm going to—

AGNES: 'Kay. Bye.

LOUISE: Bye.

LOUISE exits. She meets THERESA in the doorway as THERESA enters. LOUISE gestures to THERESA that AGNES is nuts.

THERESA: I'm back.

AGNES: That's nice.

AGNES continues to scrub as THERESA stands watching her.

THERESA: What are you trying to do, get far enough into the grain so you can count the rings?

AGNES: It's therapeutic.

THERESA: You should try getting out of the house. It's a lovely day.

AGNES: Thanks for the advice and the weather report.

THERESA: It's such a beautiful island. We so take it for granted living here, we don't really see it.

AGNES: Tell it to the Tourist Bureau.

THERESA: Ingonish. Neil's Harbour. Meat Cove, so misunderstood. And Cape North.

AGNES: What are you talking about?

THERESA: Took a little drive around this morning.

AGNES: To Cape North?

THERESA: I heard they had a nice craft shop there.

AGNES: Theresa ...

THERESA: Not a very pleasant lady running it though.

AGNES: Theresa ...

THERESA: I saw her. Joanie.

AGNES: What?

THERESA: Didn't take too long to find her. It's a small enough place. I recognized her right off by your description. She seems nice.

AGNES: What? You talked to her?

THERESA: Oh yes. A very outgoing girl.

AGNES: Who ... What ... Who did you say you were?

THERESA: I introduced myself as the sister of her friend Agnes. She mentioned that she'd missed you not being around.

AGNES: You're the limit you really are.

THERESA: Well I thought I should meet her if I'm going to be spending so much time with her.

AGNES: What?

THERESA: I think she should be here.

AGNES: Oh so what, you're stepping in to save the day?

THERESA: Agnes—

AGNES: I suggest it and it's a no, and then you decide you're going to be the good Christian—the selfless Samaritan.

THERESA: Let's not fight.

AGNES: Are you just trying to torture me? To drive me crazy?

THERESA: I prayed on it.

AGNES: Oh, and what did the Boss have to say about it?

THERESA: Nothing. Which I took as a good sign.

AGNES: I see.

THERESA: But one thing I did think was, when you get to the end of the road you can either turn around and go back the way you came—or you can make a new path.

AGNES: A new path?

THERESA: A new path.

AGNES: A path straight to Cape North.

THERESA: I just thought alright I'll go up and have a look around and see what the situation is. And you're right. It's not good.

AGNES: A week ago I wasn't capable and now all of a sudden—

THERESA: I'm not saying that you are capable, but surely between the three of us we can manage.

AGNES: Yeah well I'm not so sure anymore.

THERESA: Louise and I are her family too.

AGNES: I have to think about it.

THERESA: Well you've got 'til Saturday to think about it because that's when I said we were coming up to get her.

AGNES: What? Without asking me?

THERESA: It was your idea.

AGNES: But you said … Oh, honest to God I could just … No. No. You can't do this. You can't just turn around like that and … No. Anyway I'm thinking about going home soon. This was all just … stupid. I was stupid to think that things could work out. The damage is done and that's that. Stupid as ever.

THERESA: Agnes?

AGNES: New path my eye.

THERESA: Agnes? You're going to need a machete for this one.

AGNES: What? A machete?

THERESA: The path gets a bit thick here.

AGNES: What are you talking about?

THERESA: She's pregnant.

AGNES: What?

THERESA: She just found out. She thought she might be but she just found out for sure.

AGNES: Oh my God.

THERESA: Three months along. And she wants the baby but she's not taking care of herself. She needs some help. We have no choice but to do it. And that that … arse of a boyfriend he's just left her high and dry.

AGNES, stunned, says nothing.

THERESA: She'll be fine. We'll take care of her.

AGNES: Good Lord.

THERESA: You alright?

AGNES: I'm too young to be a grandmother.

THERESA: Well, that's what happens when you start dealing with unconventional girls. Grandma.

AGNES: Stop that. Oh my God, a grandmother. I'm not even used to being a mother yet. Oh my Lord … Is this going to work? Is this … Can we do this Theresa?

THERESA: Well I was thinking about it on the way home and I thought, sometimes God just asks you to say "whatever."

AGNES: No this is more than whatever.

THERESA: No this is exactly whatever, Grandma.

AGNES: Stop it!

THERESA: (*runs out laughing*) Grandma!

AGNES: (*running out after her*) You're evil!

THERESA: (*off*) Grandma!

AGNES: (*off*) Stop it!

Scene 6

Saturday morning. AGNES stands looking out. THERESA crosses the stage carrying sandwiches.

THERESA: Any sign?

AGNES: Not yet. What have you got there?

THERESA: Sandwiches for the drive.

THERESA exits.

AGNES: (*sarcastically*) Sure we'll make a picnic of it.

THERESA re-enters with a picnic basket.

AGNES: I'm scared out of my wits.

THERESA: That's only human.

AGNES: I've got to tell her. Who I am.

THERESA: There's no rush. You'll know when the time is right.

AGNES: I told Sandy she's coming.

THERESA: And what did Sandy say?

AGNES: Oh he started blubbering.

THERESA: That's sweet.

AGNES: More like pathetic I'd say. What's going to happen to poor Sandy?

THERESA: He'll be alright, he's got Charlie.

AGNES: Yes I guess.

AGNES looks out.

AGNES: There's someone coming now.

THERESA looks out.

THERESA: That's not Louise.

AGNES: Yes it is.

THERESA: Well what's she doing driving that big thing?

AGNES: It sure is red.

THERESA: It's huge.

LOUISE enters.

LOUISE: Isn't she beautiful!

THERESA: What is it?

LOUISE: Isn't she beautiful!

THERESA: Where's our car?

LOUISE: That's our new car.

THERESA: That's not a car.

LOUISE: It's our new truck.

THERESA: Where'd it come from?

LOUISE: I bought it off Dory.

THERESA: What?

LOUISE: Agnes said I should.

THERESA: She did?

AGNES: I did?

LOUISE: Yeah we had a talk and she said if there was something I wanted then it was right and that I'd know inside what I needed to do.

THERESA: (*to AGNES*) You did?

AGNES: Well … yes … I guess I did.

LOUISE: And you said I should get us a new car.

THERESA: That's not a car.

LOUISE: I know! Isn't she beautiful!

THERESA: I'm not going to be able to drive that rig, it's as big as a house.

LOUISE: It's easy, she handles like nothing.

THERESA: I'll feel like a farmer.

AGNES: You are a farmer.

THERESA: Oh, yes, well I suppose I am.

LOUISE: You're going to love her.

THERESA: Well come on then, truck, car, whatever, we should go if we're going.

AGNES: Oh Lord … What time did you say we'd be there?

THERESA: About four.

AGNES: Four? That's half a day away!

THERESA: Yes I know, we're going to take a little detour on the way.

AGNES: I don't know if I can handle another detour.

The women start out. They continue to talk as they exit.

LOUISE: As long as we're back in time for Theresa's show.

THERESA: It's not my show. I haven't even looked at it in days.

LOUISE: Oh it's getting really good again.

THERESA: I don't even want to know.

AGNES: Yesterday was excellent.

LOUISE: Oh yeah I love seeing Kara get hers.

THERESA: She did?

LOUISE: Yeah and good.

THERESA: Are the aliens gone?

LOUISE: Yeah they're back to real stuff now.

Scene 7

Early that afternoon. The three women stand on the beach of a river in Marion Bridge.

AGNES: Oh this isn't how I remember it at all.

THERESA: It's built up quite a bit.

AGNES: They paved the road at least.

THERESA: Look at that big place.

AGNES: Summer people probably.

LOUISE: Not much of a bridge.

THERESA: No indeed—you think if they named it after a bridge it'd be a bit nicer bridge.

AGNES: I'm sure it was a beautiful bridge before Progress got his hands on it.

THERESA: Indeed.

LOUISE: I wonder what Mother loved so much about it here?

AGNES: Not the rocky old beach that's for sure.

THERESA: No it was that.

AGNES: What?

THERESA: The sky. That day we came out and it was so beautiful at first.

LOUISE: I never came.

THERESA: No but you could've.

LOUISE: I had the chicken pox!

THERESA: Two weeks before. You were fine. You just wanted to stay home because Deena Jessome was coming over to babysit you.

LOUISE: Get outa here. I never even liked her.

THERESA: You were always following her around. What you didn't like was her boyfriends.

LOUISE: Yeah? Maybe …

THERESA: It was a lovely day.

AGNES: That's not how I remember it.

THERESA: No you were too busy chasing that poor little dog down the beach.

AGNES: That poor little dog bit me!

THERESA: Only because you were tormenting him.

AGNES: Yeah, well, he still bit me.

THERESA: It was lovely. Mother was so happy. Just staring out at the sky, lost in her dreams. But Dad didn't like that, no, he never liked seeing Mother content, and he started in on her. Just after that it started to rain. The rain followed us all the way home. And then it stopped. And then the four of us, us and Mother, we stood out in the backyard and saw the rainbow.

AGNES: Oh yeah.

LOUISE: Oh yeah.

THERESA: Filled the whole sky.

The three sisters stare into the sky.

THERESA: My goodness look at it … So big out here. Like you could just touch it.

LOUISE: Yeah.

THERESA: Just touch it like that.

LOUISE: Look at the clouds.

THERESA: Mmmm.

LOUISE: Oh look at that one!

AGNES: Which one?

LOUISE: That one there. It's a girl. See her? With her arm up?

AGNES: Oh yeah.

THERESA: Where?

AGNES: She's swimming.

THERESA: Where?

LOUISE: No she's riding a horse.

AGNES: I don't see the horse.

THERESA: I don't see the girl.

LOUISE: There. With the long hair and her arm up—and look a little smile.

THERESA: Oh yes.

AGNES: Where's the horse?

THERESA: Right under her—see that big piece is the head and—

AGNES: Oh yes I see it.

THERESA: Look at that.

LOUISE: She's happy.

AGNES: Riding away.

THERESA: She's flying.

LOUISE: She is.

AGNES: She's flying.

THERESA takes a huge pile of Post-it notes from her pocket. She hands a bunch to LOUISE.

THERESA: Here.

LOUISE: You saved them.

THERESA hands a bunch to AGNES and keeps a bunch for herself.

THERESA: To the sky. For Mother.

LOUISE: For Mother.

AGNES: For Mother.

The three women throw the notes high into the air. They stand each with an arm above their head as the notes fall around them and the lights fade.

THE END.

MARION BRIDGE

Screenplay

Marion Bridge premiered in 2002, directed by Wiebke von Carlsfeld, written by Daniel MacIvor, in an Idlewild Films Inc./Sienna Films Inc. production with the following cast:

AGNES	Molly Parker
THERESA	Rebecca Jenkins
LOUISE	Stacey Smith
ROSE	Marguerite McNeil
JOANIE	Ellen Page
CHRISSY	Hollis McLaren
DORY	Emmy Alcorn
KEN	Joseph Rutten
VALERIE	Nicola Lipman
MARLENE	Jackie Torrens
SANDY	Kevin Curran
MICKEY	Ashley MacIsaac
SUE	Heather Rankin
EVIE	Linda Busby
TAVERN BARTENDER	Stephen Manuel
AIRPORT BARTENDER	Jim Swansberg

Produced by Jennifer Kawaja, Bill Niven and Julia Sereny
Co-produced by Brent Barclay

EXT. BEACH—DAY

The sound of water. We are underwater. We rise up and see a long expanse of rocky beach.

INT. AIRPORT—LATE AFTERNOON

Sound continues. Close on the eyes of a woman. AGNES sits waiting alone in the terminal of a tiny East Coast airport. A bored SECURITY GUARD stands near the lone gate. AGNES is in her early 30s, she is a small town girl who has spent most of her life in the big city. There is something in her manner which makes one sense she has survived a terrible tragedy—or is in the midst of surviving. The way she takes up space in the world it is as if she is always making her way through a crowd, which makes her seem somehow misplaced here in this empty, small town airport. A huge, overstuffed suitcase sits beside her, in her lap is a disorganized carry-on bag. She fumbles through her carry-on looking for a cigarette. Finds it. Looks for a match. Finds it. She puts the cigarette in her mouth then looks up. The SECURITY GUARD eyes her, daring her to light the cigarette. AGNES looks at him, considering this. She looks around the room and sees a sign indicating a bar. AGNES pulls the cigarette from her mouth, rises and heads for the bar.

INT. AIRPORT BAR—LATE AFTERNOON

A BARTENDER crosses past a television which shows a beer commercial and begins checking his stock. AGNES pulls up to the bar with her luggage. She sits. The BARTENDER looks toward her expectantly.

AGNES: I'm just having a smoke.

She lights her cigarette.

BARTENDER: This area's supposed to be for patrons only.

AGNES: Yeah and I'm supposed to be living happily every after with a prince and a pony.

The BARTENDER, somewhat confused, turns away.

BARTENDER: Sure. Whatever.

After a moment AGNES puts some coins on the counter.

AGNES: Ginger ale.

INT. AIRPORT BAR—LATE AFTERNOON

Later. AGNES watches local programming on the television behind the bar. An ad for a local "Beverage Room" which places us firmly in small town Nova Scotia. Behind her we hear a voice.

THERESA: (*o.c.*) Sorry sorry sorry, we've got Louise's old bucket, first we couldn't get it started and then we couldn't get the trunk closed—

AGNES turns to face her sister THERESA. THERESA is in her late-30s, She is beautiful but hides inside the disguise of a middle-aged woman. Her hair is plainly done and she wears a bulky hand-knit sweater and loose fitting slacks.

THERESA: —and now apparently the trunk won't open. Louise is at it with a screwdriver out there now.

AGNES stands up from her seat at the bar. Her ginger ale sits untouched.

THERESA: Finish your drink if you want.

AGNES: No I'm fine.

THERESA looks down at the large suitcase.

THERESA: That's some big suitcase.

AGNES: I never know what to pack.

THERESA: Yeah me too. If I ever went anywhere I mean.

AGNES puts out her cigarette and gathers her carry-on.

THERESA: I thought you quit smoking.

AGNES: I quit a lot.

THERESA immediately takes AGNES's large suitcase and carries it banging against her legs as she leads the way out of the bar.

INT. AIRPORT—LATE AFTERNOON

Continuous action as THERESA leads AGNES out of the airport.

THERESA: Well they say it takes five or six times before it really sticks. Donnie started smoking again. "She" smokes, and with his lungs!

AGNES reaches for the suitcase.

AGNES: Here, give me that.

THERESA pulls the suitcase away from her and continues out of the airport.

THERESA: No I'm fine I'm fine.

AGNES: Theresa, it's got wheels.

THERESA: I'm fine.

THERESA continues to carry the bag, banging against her legs, as AGNES follows her.

THERESA: And don't let on you're upset we're late, Louise is all beside herself already.

AGNES: I'm not upset.

THERESA: And for God's sake don't mention her hair.

INT. CAR—DUSK

Long rays of setting sun reflect off the windows of the old sedan. Through the car's windows we see the industrial landscape of Sydney—an island city whose main industry is a steel plant which stopped making steel many years ago and whose population is steadily dropping. LOUISE, the middle sister in her mid-30s, drives her clunking old sedan. LOUISE is a sturdy,

*somewhat gruff young woman, her hair has recently
been cut in a blunt, slightly uneven bob. AGNES and
THERESA are squeezed into the front seat beside her with
THERESA in the middle. AGNES's large suitcase takes up
the backseat. The drive into the city passes through a
landscape which is strangely post-apocalyptic: empty
fields with burnt vegetation, half-built malls of which
construction has seemingly halted. The sun sets behind
the smoke stacks of the steel plant. The car stops at a
traffic light. AGNES moves to light a cigarette.*

THERESA: (*whining*) Oh Agnes …

LOUISE: (*to AGNES*) I thought you quit.

THERESA: (*to LOUISE*) She quits a lot apparently. (*to AGNES*)
Can't you wait five minutes?

AGNES: (*to LOUISE*) So what happened to your hair Louise?

LOUISE: (*to THERESA*) See! See!

THERESA: Oh for God's sake—

LOUISE: Everybody is so going to notice.

THERESA: She only noticed because I told her not to
notice.

LOUISE: Well why'd you have to tell her not to notice if
she wasn't going to?

THERESA: We'll fix it up later.

LOUISE: (*to AGNES; indicating THERESA*) *She* cut it that's
what happened to it.

THERESA: You can't cut your own hair Louise.

LOUISE: I've been cutting my own hair for years, it's never
been a problem. 'Til now. 'Til you.

*In the midst of this bickering AGNES has lit a cigarette,
she blows her smoke out the window unnoticed. The
light changes, the car pulls away.*

THERESA: We'll fix it up later.

LOUISE: You won't be doing nothing to it I can guarantee
you that.

THERESA: It's no worse than the mess you make of it.

LOUISE: Shut up.

THERESA: You shut up.

INT. KITCHEN/LIVING ROOM—EARLY EVENING

The family home. THERESA and LOUISE both still in their coats. THERESA sits at the kitchen table. LOUISE tends to her hair in a mirror near the sink with a pair of scissors. THERESA waits with some impatience. It is clear that no housekeepers live here. Dishes are piled helter-skelter on a drying rack, newspapers tower in corners, dish towels in need of laundering hang from cupboard handles, knick-knacks and wall hangings abound. The kitchen expands into the living room, or more properly the living area since it is as if this is all one big room. This area is also unkempt, it is dominated by a modern, big-screen television. There are paperbacks everywhere, old armchairs and a sofa covered in homemade afghans, a K-Mart painting of Scottish hills, a blocked-off fireplace whose mantelpiece is covered with framed photographs, ancient Christmas cards, letters to be answered, unfilled vases and more knick-knacks.

THERESA: (*calling upstairs*) It's already almost six-thirty!

INT. UPSTAIRS BEDROOMS/HALLWAY—EARLY EVENING

AGNES walks down the hallway with her suitcases. She stops for a moment and looks into THERESA's old bedroom where teenage wallpaper of yellow flowers still hangs, near the bed are a white writing desk and matching bedside table with several yearbooks and photo albums piled thereon, a frilly lamp with dusty plastic covering sits on the bedside table. By the way THERESA's clothes are hung about the room it is clear that she has been living here for some time, but refuses to imagine it's permanent. AGNES continues down the hallway and passes an overflowing chest of drawers. She pauses for a moment outside her mother's room. This is the neatest room in the house because it has been uninhabited for some time. She looks at the well-made bed in the iron bed frame, the organized night table, the small television and mountain of books—she moves quickly away. She looks into the small bathroom at the one lightbulb in the two-lightbulb socket above the mirror and the twenty-year-old pink fuzzy carpet on the floor. At the end of the hall is LOUISE's room, once the room they shared. Two single beds form an "L" in the corner of the room, the walls bare but for a crucifix and a creased poster of some ubiquitous hockey star on LOUISE's messy side of the room. AGNES places her suitcases in the corner of the room and returns to the hallway. She walks to a small closet at the end of the hall. She opens it and fishes around on a high shelf.

INT. KITCHEN—EARLY EVENING

THERESA waits impatiently. LOUISE's hair falls into the sink.

THERESA: Agnes! They start kicking visitors out at quarter to eight!

INT. HALLWAY/BEDROOM—EARLY EVENING

AGNES continues searching in the closet until she comes across a box which she takes down from the shelf. AGNES brings the box back to her room. She puts the box on her bed and opens it. In the box is a flannel shirt, under the shirt is a half-empty bottle of rye and two small flasks. She expertly fills one of the flasks and puts the bottle away.

THERESA: (*o.c.*) Agnes!

AGNES: (*calling down*) One second. I'm just changing.

INT. KITCHEN—EARLY EVENING

THERESA calls up to AGNES, LOUISE listens for her response.

THERESA: What?

AGNES: (*o.c.*) I'm changing my clothes.

Both THERESA and LOUISE, knowing immediately this is going to take some time, settle in. LOUISE takes the mirror off the wall and with her scissors heads into the living room, THERESA goes to the stove and puts on the kettle for tea. We hear the television click on in the living room.

INT. HOSPITAL—EVENING

At the hospital the three women stand around the bed of their mother, ROSE, 61. THERESA is holding a flaming birthday cake in front of ROSE. ROSE has been sick with cancer for some time and is slowly losing the battle. Clearly ROSE has been here in this room for months, we can see by the accoutrement of her daily life which sit on the bedside table and line the windowsill. Books, plants, bottles of pills, a small television, a boom box, stacks of cassette tapes. The curtain is drawn around the bed beside ROSE, behind which a woman is occasionally heard to moan. The three sisters clap their hands quietly.

THERESA: Make a wish Mother.

ROSE: (*darkly*) Oh go on, what am I supposed to wish for.

THERESA: Just anything Mother. Just wish.

ROSE: I'm not wishing anything. You wish.

THERESA: (*growing impatient*) It's your birthday.

ROSE: I've got nothing to wish for.

THERESA: Anything Mother. World peace.

ROSE: World peace. I'll world peace you. I'll tell you what I'd wish for—I wish I was back on two, I hate this third floor and— (*indicating the unseen woman in the next bed*) —rigs like that there, with their moaning and groaning all night long.

THERESA blows out the candles.

THERESA: Mother shh!

LOUISE: (*to THERESA*) What did you wish for?

THERESA: Nothing be quiet.

ROSE: And she pees the bed.

THERESA: (*sharply*) Mother!

ROSE: Well she does can't you smell it.

THERESA takes a small package from her bag.

THERESA: Here look I got you a nice … It's one of those candles you like.

She holds it under her mother's nose.

THERESA: Mmm. Nice eh? Lavender. You like lavender.

ROSE: I can't smell nothing but pee.

THERESA cuts the cake and pulls paper plates from her bag.

ROSE: (*to LOUISE*) What happened to your hair?

LOUISE shoots a look to THERESA then storms out of the room.

THERESA: Oh for God's sake.

THERESA follows LOUISE out of the room. ROSE and AGNES look at one another a moment.

ROSE: Look at you. Coming all this way. And for what?

AGNES: For you.

ROSE: (*lovingly*) Shut up.

AGNES: I brought you something.

AGNES holds up ROSE's flask.

ROSE: Oh you angel! Tell me there's a cigarette to go with it and guard the door.

INT. HOSPITAL ROOM—NIGHT

Later. ROSE fixes her hair and her makeup. She works with a small mirror and applies youthful pink lipstick to her lips and cheeks. The candle burns on the bedside table. The moon hangs in the dark blue sky. ROSE tries to keep herself from coughing as she savours the cigarette and the delicate little sips from her flask. AGNES gazes out the window, sitting on the windowsill.

ROSE: —and herself well it's sad. Donnie this, Donnie that, Donnie, Donnie. They'll be getting one of those whatchmacallits on her—a retaining order or a whatever you call it. Has she been on about the tree? Oh Lord the tree the tree. "That's my tree," she says. I said to her "Theresa it's just a tree for the love of God, there's a whole island of trees." No, she says, she says it's her tree she says. And it's not the bloody tree at all of course you know that. It's him. Just let him go is all you have to do. It's not that hard.

A silence descends between the two women, both lost in a private thought. ROSE and AGNES become aware of the silence, ROSE starts speaking again to deflect the silence.

ROSE: And Louise, did she tell you? She's getting workman's compensation. Third day in the kitchen at that new place and she puts out her back cleaning the fryer. And she's making more on compensation than she was for the two years she was on unemployment. And what's she doing with it I don't know. She's sure not spending it. She doesn't do nothing but watch that damn television.

AGNES checks her watch, she goes to the bedside table and takes a tissue from the drawer, wets it.

AGNES: Closing time. Here get rid of the evidence.

AGNES takes ROSE's cigarette from her, puts it out in the wet tissue and drops it in the wastepaper basket. She reaches for the flask.

ROSE: I'll hang onto it.

ROSE tucks the flask under her pillow. AGNES looks at ROSE and sees the pink blotches of lipstick unblended on her cheeks.

AGNES: Oh Mother, you could blend a bit.

AGNES efficiently rubs the pink colour into the skin on ROSE's face. This is the first time they have touched since AGNES arrived. The two women look at one another and in this accidental intimacy AGNES sees the fear in her mother's eyes. AGNES moves away.

AGNES: I'll go round up the girls.

EXT. HOSPITAL PARKING LOT—NIGHT

The car pulls out of the parking lot.

THERESA: (*o.c.*) So you want to get dropped somewhere?

INT. CAR—NIGHT

The three sisters sit in the car. LOUISE drives, THERESA sits up front with ROSE's cake in her lap, AGNES sits in the back.

AGNES: Like where?

THERESA: I don't know. I figured you'd be meeting some people at the bar or whatever.

AGNES: No.

LOUISE: (*to AGNES*) So are you going out later?

AGNES: No I'm just … I'm tired. I just want to go home.

LOUISE gives THERESA a look like "what's up with her," THERESA shrugs her shoulders and shakes her head as if to say "who knows." AGNES leans back looking out the window at the coloured lights of the small town city.

AGNES: (*almost to herself*) I just want to go home.

INT. LIVING ROOM—NIGHT

Later that night. LOUISE sits in front of the television which broadcasts a bad American sitcom. LOUISE has a mirror leaning on the table in front of her as she continues to pick at her haircut with a pair of scissors. Beyond her we see AGNES sitting at the kitchen table.

INT. KITCHEN—NIGHT

AGNES sits at the kitchen table drinking tea and smoking a cigarette. THERESA enters the kitchen, she is dressed for bed, she puts on the kettle for tea. AGNES moves to put out her cigarette.

AGNES: (*re: cigarette*) Sorry ...

THERESA: Oh whatever. I guess if you can be smoking up the hospital with Mother you can be smoking here.

AGNES puts out her cigarette.

AGNES: So what are your plans, you're moving back in here?

THERESA: Well ... I mean ... For now. Until Donnie comes to his senses. Living at the hotel was just getting to be too expensive. And there's room here. (*re: LOUISE*) She likes the company anyway, though she wouldn't let on. (*after a moment*) What about you? How long are you staying?

AGNES: I don't know. I'm kind of ... flexible right now.

THERESA: Oh yeah. You still at that same restaurant?

AGNES: I'm taking a bit of a break.

THERESA: Another "holiday" is it?

AGNES: Not really ...

THERESA: (*quietly*) It's not going to be the go like it was when you were here last Christmas. Sketchy types coming and going in and out of here all hours of the night and day. (*re: LOUISE*) You had her scared half out of her wits.

AGNES: Oh please she's not a baby.

THERESA: No no, there's no question as to who the baby is.

AGNES moves to rise.

THERESA: Stay as long as you want, stay a week, stay two. But don't be starting any trouble.

AGNES: No.

THERESA: You promise?

AGNES: Yes.

The kettle boils. AGNES rises and leaves.

AGNES: Good night.

EXT. HOUSE—MORNING

A big orange sun rises behind the house. A simple two-storey wooden structure in dire need of a paint job. The front door never gets used, occasionally someone may sit on the front steps, but to do this they would come from the main entrance which is a side door leading from the kitchen to the driveway.

INT. KITCHEN—MORNING

Quietly AGNES picks up the car keys and slips out of the house careful not to wake anyone.

EXT. HOUSE—MORNING

AGNES slips out of the house and into the car. Next door EVIE MACLELLAN, 55, big and curious, peeks out her front window, her tiny dog in her arms. AGNES backs out of the driveway.

INT. CAR—DAY

AGNES drives along the highway in the sedan. She smokes nervously, the radio turned up loud.

EXT. HIGHWAY—DAY

The car whizzes along the highway out of the industrial city and into the bucolic countryside.

EXT. TOWN MAIN STREET—DAY

The main street of a small town of approximately a thousand people. In appearance it rides the fine line between delightful and depressing. Wooden and brick storefronts—many abandoned, flat-roofed houses, dirt roads leading up and down from the main street, a prominent church and gas station. AGNES sits in the car on the main road across from the brightly decorated Chrissy's Craft Shop. It is a wooden building filled with sun-catchers and woven items. AGNES watches the store.

Through the front window she notices a young woman working in the shop. She studies her carefully. This is JOANIE, 15, tall and thin, a tight-fitting T-shirt and jeans. She looks very much as AGNES might have looked at that age. Trying to look inconspicuous AGNES slides over to the passenger side to get a better look. JOANIE exits the shop and leans against the front wall of the building. AGNES slides back behind the wheel of the car. A woman's voice (CHRISSY) calls from inside the shop.

CHRISSY: (*o.c.*) Joanie!

JOANIE lights a cigarette as she notices AGNES pull quickly away in the car. CHRISSY calls out again.

CHRISSY: (*o.c.*) Joanie!

JOANIE looks distractedly away.

INT. CAR—DAY

AGNES picks up speed as she pulls out of the town. She nervously fumbles with lighting a cigarette.

INT. KITCHEN—DAY

LOUISE stands in the kitchen with her coat on, waiting impatiently. AGNES enters.

LOUISE: Where the heck were you?

AGNES: Nowhere.

THERESA enters the kitchen, her coat on.

THERESA: (*to LOUISE*) There see, it's not the end of the world, she's back. I told you. (*to AGNES*) Where were you?

AGNES: Nowhere. Just cruising around.

LOUISE grabs the keys from AGNES.

AGNES: Sorry. I didn't realize you had somewhere to be.

LOUISE: We got our prayer meeting. Which we nearly missed.

THERESA heads out the door.

THERESA: We didn't nearly miss it, we're fine on time.

AGNES: You're going now?

LOUISE: We should've been gone fifteen minutes ago.

THERESA: (*to LOUISE*) Well shut up and come on then.

AGNES: I'll come too.

THERESA and LOUISE are frozen in their tracks.

THERESA: What?

AGNES: I'll come. Can I come?

LOUISE: To the prayer meeting?

AGNES: Yeah.

LOUISE: Why?

AGNES: You don't want me to?

THERESA: No come on come on. You might want to grab an umbrella there Louise.

LOUISE: What for?

THERESA: You never know what kind of a mess is going to be coming down with the pigs flying today.

LOUISE guffaws as they head out the door.

LOUISE: That's for sure.

We hear a group of people singing and praying.

EXT. CHURCH HALL—DAY

Voices come from a small simply built brick and concrete building that serves as a church hall. Several kilometres outside the city. A small dirt parking lot holds a few cars including the sedan. A souped up red truck pulls into the lot, a woman (DORY) gets out and heads into the hall.

INT. CHURCH HALL—DAY

A brightly coloured children's drawing of the Virgin Mary crying as she watches Christ's ascension into heaven. Wooden stacking tables line one wall, the room is decorated with children's drawings made here when the room becomes a Sunday school. A circle of folding chairs in the centre of the room where a DOZEN PEOPLE sing and pray. Most of these are women. One man, CHARLIE, seems to be the leader. His eyes are closed and his head is bowed, his lips move quickly and quietly in prayer, one hand is held aloft while the other fingers a lace of rosary beads. Some people are standing, holding both arms in the air and swaying in prayer. One WOMAN is singing a hymn. Some people join in for a line or two and others punctuate the song with little shouts of "Amen" and "Praise the Lord." ANOTHER WOMAN speaks quietly in tongues. THERESA sits with her eyes closed and her hands in the air before her. She wears an expression of deep concentration as if waiting for something to happen. LOUISE has her eyes closed, her lips pressed tightly together. The woman from the truck, DORY, enters and takes a seat beside LOUISE. DORY is a handsome woman, mid-30s, wearing slacks and a blazer over a crisp white shirt. DORY's voice rises above the others in her shouts of praise. AGNES takes it all in while trying not to be too conspicuously the observer. The song peters out into an ending.

CHARLIE: Praise the Lord and praise our Holy Mother Mary Queen of Heaven, that she may be with us in our time of need and lead us to the path of salvation. Special prayers today for the soul of Malcolm Vickers, recently gone to glory and for the health and salvation of our own Rose MacKeigan. Blessed be the weak of heart, blessed be the meek, blessed be the pious, blessed be the virtuous.

The group continues to pray. The WOMAN continues to speak in tongues, loudly and with great conviction. DORY reaches over and takes LOUISE's hand tightly in her own. AGNES sees this and finds it deeply significant while the rest of the group take no special notice. The WOMAN continues to speak in tongues then stops, exhausted. CHARLIE who has been listening to her interprets for the group.

CHARLIE: The way of the Lord is right and wise, trust in him, and he will bring us home.

EXT. CHURCH HALL PARKING LOT—DAY

AGNES and THERESA arrive at the car as the last of the meeting trickles out of the parking lot. AGNES lights a cigarette and looks back toward the hall and sees LOUISE and DORY chatting. THERESA tries to open the passenger door of the sedan but it is locked.

THERESA: Why in the name of God she locks it in a church parking lot, it's not like it's New York or something.

AGNES: (*indicating DORY*) Who's that?

THERESA: (*looking back*) She's a Ferguson. They run the dairy out by the reserve.

THERESA and AGNES watch DORY and LOUISE. DORY puts her hand on LOUISE's shoulder, LOUISE laughs. THERESA watches AGNES watching DORY and LOUISE.

THERESA: Agnes? What?

AGNES: What? Nothing.

THERESA calls to LOUISE.

THERESA: (*indicating the car door is locked*) Louise!

LOUISE bids DORY goodbye. DORY gives LOUISE a hug and heads off to her truck. AGNES smiles at this. THERESA catches the smile.

THERESA: (*to AGNES*) What?

AGNES: Nothing. What?

AGNES smiles and leans against the car.

THERESA: (*impatiently*) Louise!

INT. HOSPITAL ROOM—DAY

ROSE sits up in bed. She is weak but eager to hide it. LOUISE stands near the door. THERESA hovers, looking for something to do while AGNES fusses with her mother's pillows. The curtains are drawn on the next bed, quiet moans are heard there from time to time.

THERESA: (*to AGNES*) I'll do that.

AGNES: That's okay.

ROSE: (*to AGNES*) So what? Did you sit in the car?

THERESA: No she came into the meeting and everything.

While at the pillows AGNES expertly replaces the hidden, spent flask with a second. ROSE gives AGNES a little wink.

ROSE: Praise the Lord.

THERESA busies herself with arranging the bedside table.

ROSE: And who all else was there?

THERESA: The usual suspects.

ROSE: Was what's her name there with her tongues? That all seems a bit of a show to me.

THERESA: Now Mother, it's not for us to judge. Charlie remembered you in our prayers.

ROSE: God bless him. There's not many like him.

AGNES: Louise's friend was there.

LOUISE: Who?

AGNES: With the fancy truck.

ROSE: Oh the Ferguson. She's got an excellent memory. She knows the name of every patron saint in order of what they're patron of.

AGNES: (*to LOUISE*) She seemed like a nice lady.

LOUISE: (*laughing at the word "lady"*) She's not a lady.

AGNES: What is she then?

LOUISE: I don't know.

AGNES: You were having a good talk.

LOUISE: She was just telling me about trying to sell her truck.

AGNES: We should have her over for dinner sometime.

THERESA: What?

LOUISE: I'm going to get a pop.

AGNES: No wait Louise.

LOUISE: You have her over for dinner if you want.

AGNES: No I mean, we all need to have a talk about something.

THERESA and LOUISE look terrified, the last thing they want to do is "have a talk," with "talking" conflict seems inevitable. Even ROSE looks a little worried.

THERESA: Do you like that lavender candle Mother?

ROSE: Oh yes it's nice. But you know I prefer the fruitier ones.

THERESA: Like the raspberry I got you before?

ROSE: No. Like apple or pear or something.

THERESA: I've never seen pear.

AGNES: (*pointedly*) Can we have a talk?

ROSE: Talk then talk, go ahead and talk.

The room becomes silent. All wait for the words.

AGNES: Well, Mother I'm thinking that maybe it's time you came home.

ROSE: Don't be foolish. What do you mean?

AGNES: I talked to your doctor—

THERESA: What doctor?

AGNES: Mother's doctor.

LOUISE: When?

AGNES: On the way in. (*to ROSE*) And she said that if there was someone there to keep an eye on you there's no reason you couldn't come home.

THERESA: Well that's all fine but whose eye is that supposed to be, I'm working four days a week for Father Dan and— (*indicating LOUISE*) —with her back this one can barely lift the remote control.

AGNES: I'd be there. I'll stay. (*to ROSE*) I'll stay home.

THERESA and LOUISE are dumbstruck. The WOMAN in the next bed moans.

THERESA: Don't be ridiculous Agnes—

AGNES: I want to.

THERESA: But—

AGNES: It's what does Mother want. (*to ROSE*) Mother? What do you want?

ROSE looks at her daughters. The WOMAN in the next bed continues to moan. ROSE's eyes fill with tears as she looks at AGNES.

ROSE: I want to come home.

AGNES: Then that's that. You'll come home.

EXT. HOSPITAL PARKING LOT—DAY

LOUISE approaches the car. THERESA angrily strides along behind her followed by AGNES.

THERESA: "And that's that. You'll come home." You're something else.

AGNES: You don't want Mother home?

THERESA: That's not what I'm saying, I'm saying who's going to take care of her.

AGNES: I am.

THERESA: You are!? That's a joke.

LOUISE arrives at the car but doesn't stop and keeps walking.

THERESA: (*to LOUISE*) Where are you going?

LOUISE tosses the car keys to THERESA.

LOUISE: (*calling back*) I'm walking.

THERESA catches the keys.

AGNES: Theresa? I stopped drinking.

THERESA: What about the drugs?

AGNES: Everything.

THERESA: Yeah, for the hundred and what'dth time?

AGNES: I've been sixty-five days sober.

THERESA: Oh for God's sake Agnes who are you trying to kid? I can smell it off you now.

AGNES: That's the flask I brought for Mother, it was leaking in my bag.

THERESA takes a long look at AGNES.

THERESA: Oh yeah, you're going to take some good care of her aren't you.

THERESA follows off behind LOUISE walking. She tosses the keys to AGNES.

THERESA: (*o.c.*) (*calling after her*) Hang on Louise I'm coming with you.

AGNES catches the keys. She watches her sisters walk away. In anger AGNES kicks the car tire.

AGNES: Christ.

EXT. HOSPITAL PARKING LOT—DUSK

A dozen cigarette butts lie crushed on the ground near the sedan's front tire. AGNES sits on the hood of the car smoking as she has been doing for some time. The parking lot is nearly empty. She drops her cigarette on the ground and crushes it with her foot. She slides off the hood and gets into the car.

INT. CAR—DUSK

AGNES drives along the streets of Sydney looking for a telephone. She tries to find some music on the radio. The only choice seems to be between New Country and Early Eighties. She goes for the Eighties. She turns onto the main drag. Young people gather pointlessly on corners. Cars cruise along aimlessly. Empty for-rent storefronts, bars, pizza places. This is as bright lights big city as Sydney gets. She parks near a tavern and sits in the car a moment. She gets out of the car.

EXT. PHONE BOOTH—NIGHT

AGNES stands in a phone booth talking on a pay phone. She is leaving a message on her AA sponsor's telephone voice mail.

AGNES: (*on phone*) Hey Sharon, it's Angie. Just wanted to let you know I got in okay. Things are good, everybody's, you know, pleased that I'm going to be staying, and all that. I haven't found a meeting yet, but I'm getting on that tomorrow. And that's it I guess, say hi to everybody at the group and you can call me at ... You know what actually, I'll call you. Okay. Bye bye. And you're right, I don't miss Toronto one bit.

AGNES hangs up the phone.

AGNES: Fuck.

She turns and sees a tavern.

INT. TAVERN—NIGHT

AGNES enters the mid-sized tavern. Wood panelling. Multiple television sets. A long wooden bar where a few patrons sit: A COUPLE of all day REGULARS. A drunk man, SANDY, 35, and a heavily made-up woman, MARLENE, 32, sit at one end of the bar. At the back of the room is a jukebox near a tiny makeshift dance floor. THREE COUPLES populate the mostly empty tables scattered throughout the room. AGNES nervously moves through the room taking in the details. She looks into the jukebox reading the song titles, trying to be casual. A WOMAN calls from the bar.

MARLENE: Agnes?

AGNES turns and looks.

MARLENE: Oh my God girl I heard you got home yesterday, where were you last night?

AGNES approaches MARLENE and SANDY at the bar.

MARLENE: Look Sandy it's Agnes.

AGNES: Hey Marlene.

MARLENE: Oh God love you, there's been frig all happening since you left last Christmas. Look Sandy it's Agnes. He wouldn't believe you were home 'cause you weren't here.

AGNES: Hi Sandy.

SANDY: (*blearily*) Yeah yeah, good good.

MARLENE: Sorry about your mom, I heard they moved her up to the third floor.

AGNES: Where'd you hear that?

MARLENE: Evie MacLellan next door to you, her sister works on three.

AGNES: She's going to be coming home.

MARLENE: Who? Your mom?

AGNES: Yeah. Home to the house.

MARLENE: (*darkly*) Oh you mean for the duration or whatever?

AGNES: Or whatever, yeah.

MARLENE: That's sad.

SANDY: What's sad?

MARLENE: Agnes's mom.

SANDY: Oh that's sad.

AGNES: Uh huh.

MARLENE: And it's hard.

SANDY: It's fucking hard too.

MARLENE: So what's the big news up Toronto? See any concerts?

SANDY starts to weep.

SANDY: It's fucking hard.

MARLENE: For the love of God Sandy get it together.

SANDY: Fuck off Marlene.

MARLENE: Don't you fucking tell me to fuck off.

SANDY: You bet I can fucking tell you to fuck off in my fucking house.

MARLENE: We're in the tavern you arsehole.

SANDY: Yeah. Well so whatever. Fuck you.

AGNES slips out as they continue to argue.

MARLENE: Fuck you Sandy.

SANDY: Fuck you yourself.

MARLENE: (*noticing AGNES has left; to SANDY*) Sandy you're scaring people away again. (*calling to BARTENDER*) Two tequila shooters and a glass of water.

EXT. HOUSE—NIGHT

The sedan pulls into the driveway. AGNES gets out of the car and walks toward the house. Next door EVIE MACLELLAN peeks out from behind her kitchen curtains. AGNES spots her and immediately strides toward EVIE's prying eye.

AGNES: How are you tonight Evie?

EVIE opens her door a crack and pokes her head out, her little mop of a dog squirms in her arms. AGNES stands at the bottom of EVIE's steps.

EVIE: Oh Agnes it's good to see you home again so soon. Your poor dear mother must be so happy. I heard they moved her up to the third floor. There's not many get off three.

AGNES: She's coming home actually.

EVIE: She's coming home?

AGNES: Didn't you hear? They found the cure for cancer.

EVIE: Oh I see.

AGNES: Bye then Evie.

AGNES all smiles heads into the house.

EVIE: Yes right. Bye.

INT. KITCHEN—NIGHT

AGNES enters the kitchen. THERESA sits at the table reading the paper. In the living room we can hear a romantic drama LOUISE is watching. AGNES passes through the room to go upstairs.

THERESA: Hey.

AGNES stops.

THERESA: I was on the phone this evening to some places. Tomorrow they'll be delivering a hospital bed and one of them tables that goes up and down. And a bedpan. Who's going to handle the bedpan that's what I want to know.

AGNES: (*softly, smiling*) I'll handle the bedpan.

THERESA: We'll all handle the bedpan.

LOUISE: (*o.c.*) I'm not going near no bedpan.

INT. KITCHEN—DAY

The next day. AGNES does a huge pile of dishes.

INT. LIVING ROOM—DAY

AGNES gathers piles of newspapers and bundles them with string.

INT. BATHROOM—DAY

AGNES cleans the bathroom.

INT. ROSE'S BEDROOM—DAY

AGNES finishes disassembling her mother's bed, leaning the bed frame against the wall. She opens the closet to clean there and comes upon an ancient wooden box on a shelf. AGNES sits on the floor and opens the box which is filled with photographs. AGNES looks through the photographs: various Cape Breton vistas, Rose on a camping trip, Rose at a party, Theresa dressed for the prom with a date, Louise in hockey gear, the three sisters as girls on a beach, Louise and Theresa as teenage girls in birthday hats in front of a birthday cake, Agnes alone as a fifteen-year-old looking very much like Joanie.

INT. KITCHEN—DAY

AGNES on her hands and knees with a bucket and a brush, scrubs the kitchen floor. LOUISE enters the kitchen from outside with a sandwich from a sub shop and a can of pop. She continues into the living room. She looks around at the neatness.

LOUISE: Where are my papers?

AGNES: I bundled them up.

LOUISE: I got stuff in them I'm saving.

AGNES: They're in the basement.

LOUISE: They better not get dirty down there.

LOUISE flops onto the sofa and turns on the television and begins surfing. She settles on a nature show. AGNES rises from the floor and retrieves a small pile of photos from the counter.

AGNES: Louise, come here, look at this.

LOUISE: My show's on.

AGNES walks into the living room.

INT. LIVING ROOM—DAY

AGNES sits on the sofa beside LOUISE who keeps her attention on the television and her sandwich.

AGNES: I found these in Mother's room.

She holds a photo out to LOUISE.

AGNES: Mother at the beach. Remember that silly hat.

LOUISE glances quickly at the photo. AGNES looks at another then shows it to LOUISE.

AGNES: I just turned fifteen there.

LOUISE doesn't look at the photo. AGNES offers another.

AGNES: And here's your birthday. Look how skinny you were.

LOUISE takes the photo and looks at it.

AGNES: You were seventeen. I know because I wasn't there. That was the Marion Bridge summer.

LOUISE hands the photo back to AGNES.

LOUISE: I don't like all this past stuff.

AGNES: Oh.

LOUISE: My show's on.

AGNES: Fine.

AGNES rises with the photos and leaves the room.

INT. KITCHEN—DAY

AGNES throws the photos on the kitchen table and returns to scrubbing the floor.

INT. LIVING ROOM—NIGHT

That night. ANGLE ON: the television screen, two lovers in a heated clinch. LOUISE passively watches the screen. We hear the door open into the kitchen.

INT. KITCHEN—NIGHT

THERESA enters the sparkling clean kitchen from outside.

THERESA: Aren't the days supposed to be getting longer? It's already dark as midnight. (*noticing the room*) Somebody sure broke out the elbow grease in here. Isn't this great? Where is she?

LOUISE: Out back.

THERESA notices the photos on the kitchen table, she picks them up and looks at them.

THERESA: Where did these come from?

LOUISE: She found them cleaning up.

THERESA quietly puts the photos in a drawer under some pamphlets and old bills. She looks out the window.

EXT. BACKYARD—NIGHT

AGNES sits in a lawn chair in the moonlight smoking. THERESA comes around the corner. She sits in a chair near AGNES.

THERESA: Looks great in there. Hasn't had a clean like that in years. Do you keep your place in Toronto neat like that?

AGNES: Oh you know, it's easier if it's somebody else's.

THERESA: Yes it's true, after a day of cleaning for Father Dan it's the last thing I want to do when I get home. (*hearing herself; realizing this has become her home again*) "Home." (*a beat*) It's chilly.

AGNES: It's nice though.

THERESA: Yes.

AGNES: (*looking up at the stars*) All the time we spent out here.

THERESA: We sat out here a lot, we did.

AGNES: Hiding from Dad. Wishing on the stars.

THERESA: (*quietly*) We're not getting into all that are we?

AGNES: (*into the sky*) "Star light star bright … "

THERESA: Is that what we're dragging Mother home into?

AGNES: " … first star I see tonight … "

THERESA: Agnes?

AGNES: " … I wish I may I wish I might … "

THERESA: Are we?

AGNES looks at THERESA.

AGNES: No.

THERESA, relieved, continues on as if nothing out of the ordinary had been said.

THERESA: Father Dan's giving me the afternoon off so I'll be here when Mother arrives.

AGNES: Okay.

THERESA rises and heads back into the house.

THERESA: I'm going to put the tea on.

THERESA leaves AGNES alone.

AGNES: (*into the sky*) " … have the wish I wish tonight."

INT. ROSE'S BEDROOM—DAY

The next day. A hospital bed and table have replaced the old iron frame and the room has been cleaned from the floor to the ceiling. AGNES finishes adding a colourful quilt to the hospital bed. From downstairs we hear the hysterical sounds of an American game show on the television. AGNES calls downstairs.

AGNES: Louise? Louise?

LOUISE: (*o.c.*) What?

AGNES: Come here for a minute.

LOUISE: (*o.c.*) My show's on.

INT. LIVING ROOM—DAY

LOUISE sits in her now familiar position in front of the television. After a moment AGNES enters holding a metal bedpan.

AGNES: Louise? Do you know what this is?

LOUISE: What?

AGNES: This is a bedpan. It's something you will become very familiar with.

LOUISE: No I won't.

AGNES: Oh yes you will.

LOUISE: Who all of a sudden made you the boss of everything?

AGNES: I'm just trying to tell you—

LOUISE: I'm not taking orders from you.

AGNES: What I'm doing is—

LOUISE: What you're doing is coming here so you can cause a big ruckus and get everybody all upset and then just take off.

AGNES: That's not what I'm doing.

LOUISE: It's what you always done before.

THERESA: (*o.c.*) (*calling from outside*) They're here, they're here.

LOUISE rises and walks past her sister and outside.

EXT. HOUSE—DAY

AGNES joins LOUISE, on the steps at the side of the house. THERESA stands in the driveway watching as ROSE stands batting away TWO AMBULANCE ATTENDANTS. A stretcher sits abandoned nearby, ROSE is having none of that. With great difficulty ROSE moves towards the steps.

ROSE: I'm telling you right now there's no way I'm getting carried into my own house. They can carry me out but they ain't carrying me in.

Next door EVIE MACLELLAN and her little dog peek out the window around the curtains. ROSE catches sight of her but ignores her. ROSE has now reached the bottom step.

THERESA: (*taking her mother's arm*) Let me give you a hand now Mother.

ROSE: (*to THERESA*) I need a clump of soil.

THERESA: A what?

ROSE: A clump of soil, get me a clump of soil.

THERESA leans down and picks up a hard lump of dirt and offers it to her mother. ROSE takes it and discards it.

ROSE: No that's too hard. Needs to be moister than that. There, that one by your foot.

THERESA gets the soil ROSE refers to and hands it to her mother.

ROSE: Perfect.

ROSE takes the clump and flings it at EVIE MACLELLAN's house, hitting the wall near the window from which EVIE peers. EVIE quickly darts back away from the window.

ROSE: Perfect!

ROSE stumbles and nearly falls over. The ATTENDANTS jump to attention, AGNES grabs her other arm, LOUISE steps forward. The group practically carries her up the steps.

ROSE: Don't crowd me, don't crowd me.

INT. ROSE'S BEDROOM—DAY

ROSE lies in bed exhausted. AGNES gives her mother a pill and a glass of water.

ROSE: This is lovely dear. All is as it should be, eh my dear. All is as it should be.

ROSE sighs and slowly drifts off to sleep. AGNES seems anxious. She quietly slips out of the room.

INT. THERESA'S BEDROOM—DAY

THERESA lies sleeping on her bed. AGNES looks into the room from the hallway then walks away.

INT. LIVING ROOM—DAY

LOUISE sits drowsily in front of a soap opera. AGNES looks in at her as she quietly makes her way through the kitchen.

INT. KITCHEN—DAY

Strains of soap opera music are heard as AGNES picks up the car keys from the counter and heads out the door.

EXT. CHRISSY'S CRAFT SHOP—DAY

The sedan parked across the street from the craft shop.

INT. CAR—DAY

AGNES sits in the car. She lights a cigarette. She exhales deeply. Across the street JOANIE exits the shop and leans against the building as she lights a cigarette. She notices AGNES sitting in the car. AGNES tries to act casual. JOANIE eyes her suspiciously. AGNES realizes that JOANIE is watching. With a feigned casualness AGNES puts out her cigarette and gets out of the car.

EXT. TOWN MAIN STREET—DAY

AGNES walks purposefully toward the tiny convenience store she happens to be parked in front of. She tries to open the door. It is locked. She tugs again. She looks in the window. She sees that the store is empty. She checks her watch and looks around. JOANIE is still watching. With as much casual energy as she can muster she goes back to her car and drives away.

EXT. HOUSE—DAY

Later that day. A loud, mournful, fiddle lament. In the backyard AGNES struggles frantically to hang white sheets on the clothesline against a hearty wind.

INT. KITCHEN/LIVING ROOM—DAY

The fiddle continues from upstairs. Pots fizz and sizzle on the stove as AGNES attempts to attack yesterday's dishes in the sink. The kitchen has begun to slip back into its former state. LOUISE is slumped as usual in front of the television which jumps from world to world ceaselessly, the sound of which fights with the fiddle coming from ROSE's boom box upstairs. THERESA passes through the room with her coat on.

AGNES: Could you get Mother to turn that down a bit do you think?

AGNES turns off the stove and prepares ROSE's lunch.

THERESA: That is turned down. (*to LOUISE*) Are you driving me or am I taking the car?

AGNES: So is this a regular thing?

THERESA: We just get together and talk once in a while. Louise?

AGNES: Does "She" know?

THERESA: She who? Louise!!

LOUISE: What?

AGNES: "She." The girlfriend.

THERESA: What about her?

AGNES: (*to THERESA*) Does she know that you and Donnie get together to talk?

THERESA: (*to AGNES*) I wouldn't know would I? (*to LOUISE*) Are you driving me or am I taking the car? Louise I'm talking to you. Louise!

LOUISE: My show's on.

THERESA: You don't watch one of them long enough to have a show Louise.

THERESA moves to exit.

THERESA: (*to LOUISE*) Where are the keys?

AGNES: (*to THERESA*) Oh I've got them here ...

AGNES takes them from her pocket and hands them to THERESA.

THERESA: Where were you with the car?

AGNES: Nowhere. Good luck. Or whatever.

THERESA: Thanks. Or whatever.

THERESA exits.

INT. KITCHEN/LIVING ROOM—DAY

Later. LOUISE in front of the TV. AGNES doing dishes at the sink, she calls to LOUISE.

AGNES: Louise, check and see if Mother ate her lunch.

LOUISE does not respond. AGNES has had enough of this, she goes into the living room and stands in front of LOUISE.

AGNES: Louise, did you hear me?

LOUISE: What?

AGNES moves in front of the television.

LOUISE: Hey! Move.

AGNES: No.

LOUISE: I'm watching that okay.

AGNES: Watch this!

AGNES grabs the remote control from LOUISE's hand, turns off the television and dashes out of the room. LOUISE dashes after her.

LOUISE: Gimmie that.

AGNES: We're taking a break.

LOUISE: It's my TV, I paid for it.

AGNES: We're taking a break.

LOUISE chases AGNES through the kitchen and out the door.

EXT. HOUSE—DAY

LOUISE chases AGNES around the house. It is becoming a game now.

LOUISE: Gimmie that.

AGNES: I'm not giving it you'll have to get it.

LOUISE: Don't you worry I'll get it.

Next door EVIE MACLELLAN watches as LOUISE chases AGNES shrieking and laughing back into the house.

INT. LIVING ROOM—DAY

LOUISE tackles AGNES and they land in a heap on the living room sofa.

AGNES: Your back seems fine to me.

LOUISE: It's just bending down, I'm okay for tackling.

They laugh.

AGNES: Don't be mad at me.

LOUISE: I'm not mad at you I'm just ...

AGNES: An old crank?

LOUISE grabs for the remote, AGNES leaps up shrieking. They struggle yelling and laughing. We hear yelling from upstairs.

ROSE: (*o.c.*) Could you please keep down the din!?

AGNES and LOUISE grow immediately quiet. Covering their mouths. Stifling their laughter like girls. Slowly they sit. They grow still. AGNES hands LOUISE the remote. LOUISE turns on the TV. After a moment:

ROSE: (*calling down*) Or bring it up here where it belongs.

INT. ROSE'S BEDROOM—DAY

A sprightly fiddle tune. ROSE sits up in bed with a drink in her hand. LOUISE leans against the door, a drink in her hand. AGNES sits on the bed.

ROSE: And what do you suppose she's doing with him now? I'd put good money on not talking.

LOUISE: Oh Mother stop it.

ROSE: You can talk on the phone, you don't need to see somebody to talk to them.

LOUISE: Leave it be Mother.

ROSE: I never liked that Donnie.

LOUISE: It's none of our business.

ROSE: What she ever saw in him I'll never know.

AGNES: Love is blind.

ROSE: It's nothing to do with love. Unless you mean making love.

LOUISE: Mother …

ROSE: Oh whatever. Who cares anyway give us another drink and turn up the fiddle.

ROSE pours herself another drink. LOUISE looks like she is about to protest.

ROSE: You're not getting out to your bowling these days Louise?

LOUISE: Not so much.

ROSE: You should, you're looking a bit puffy.

AGNES: You're bowling?

LOUISE: Nah.

ROSE: Oh she's really good. They were all looking for her to be on their teams.

LOUISE: They were not.

ROSE: Five or six different ones. The phone never stopped. She's popular in bowling. Have a drink Agnes.

AGNES: I don't think so Mother.

ROSE quickly gets a glass from the table beside her and pours AGNES a drink.

ROSE: Oh have a drink, have a drink. But just one see. That's the thing with you. You just have to tell yourself one and stick to it. Or four. In my case it's four and I know it and I stick to it.

AGNES: No Mother, not right now.

ROSE pours her drink into her own glass.

ROSE: Fine then fine.

A particularly fine bit of fiddle playing emits from the boom box.

ROSE: Listen to that girls. The fingers on that fella eh? The fingers on him.

AGNES cocks an eyebrow at LOUISE. LOUISE laughs.

INT. KITCHEN—NIGHT

Fiddling continues upstairs. AGNES pulls two trays of ice cubes from the freezer and turns to see THERESA standing in the doorway.

THERESA: What are you doing?

AGNES: (*feeling caught*) Grabbing some ice cubes.

THERESA: For Mother?

AGNES: (*adamantly*) Yes.

THERESA: Well grab some for me too.

THERESA moves to head upstairs. AGNES follows.

AGNES: You might want to fix your shirt first, you've got it on inside out.

THERESA quickly checks. AGNES was kidding.

THERESA: It is not.

AGNES: But you checked.

They head up the stairs.

THERESA: (*o.c.*) Oh stop it.

AGNES: (*o.c.*) But you checked.

THERESA: (*o.c.*) Brat.

INT. ROSE'S BEDROOM—NIGHT

The party winds down. A sad Cape Breton tune on the boom box, ROSE is drifting, well past her four-drink limit, LOUISE maintains position at the door nursing her drink, THERESA sits on the bed staring into her drink. AGNES watches THERESA. The song ends.

ROSE: Put that one on again Louise.

THERESA: No Mother now, that's the night.

ROSE: No no ... You know what would be perfect, help me outside and we'll sit in the yard for a while.

THERESA: It's getting late Mother.

ROSE: Just for a second.

AGNES: It's a bit chilly, we'll do that when it warms up a bit.

ROSE: All right all right. Let me have one of my pills then Theresa.

THERESA: No Mother.

ROSE: Just one.

THERESA: Not when you've been drinking Mother.

ROSE: What are you talking about?

THERESA: You've had a lot to drink Mother.

ROSE: Oh I've had twice this to drink and taken three.

THERESA: No Mother.

ROSE: Theresa now don't aggravate me.

LOUISE: I'm off to bed.

THERESA: Do you feel like going for a spin Louise?

LOUISE: I been drinking.

THERESA: Oh you only ever have one, that big (*indicates small*) and with three ice cubes in it.

AGNES: (*to THERESA*) I'll drive. Where do you want to go?

THERESA: I guess. Are you all right to be driving?

ROSE: Theresa I won't sleep without a pill.

THERESA: I'll give you half.

AGNES: (*to THERESA*) Where do you need to go? (*to LOUISE*) Where does she need to go?

LOUISE: (*rolls her finger by the side of her head to indicate to AGNES that THERESA is nuts*)

LOUISE leaves the room.

ROSE: Oh half's not going to do no good.

INT. CAR—NIGHT

AGNES and THERESA sit in the car across the street from a one-storey bungalow with a well-tended front yard in a residential area of similar houses and lawns. The house is illuminated by a light above the front door. THERESA never takes her gaze from the house. Occasionally a light will flick on or off inside the house. AGNES watches her sister with concern.

THERESA: —what I should have done is just not budged, but it all came on so fast and I just wanted no part of it. And you know years ago, when we first got the house Mother was all: "Make sure your name's on the mortgage," but you know at the time that just seemed like, I don't know, expecting trouble or something.

A MALE FIGURE opens the door of the house and calls for a cat. THERESA freezes, terrified to be seen. The MALE FIGURE retreats into the house.

THERESA: He used to be allergic to cats but she's got two.

A light comes on in the house.

THERESA: Somebody's in the bathroom. They put in a new tub. The old tub was fine. Look at those sad little pansies—they're an embarrassment. And that's the thing about the tree—I put that little sapling in out back myself last summer. It's my darn tree. But She says it'll kill it to dig it up.

The light in the house goes off.

THERESA: Oh. Done in the bathroom. The tree's going to die under her anyway.

A light comes on in the house.

THERESA: Oh. Somebody's going to bed. (*Pause.*) The tree's got no hope—look at those pansies.

The light above the front door goes off. Finally the house is in darkness. AGNES starts up the car and pulls away. THERESA watches the house disappear behind her.

INT. KITCHEN—NIGHT

Later. AGNES sits alone in the dimly lit kitchen. Everyone else is sleeping. She talks on the telephone, leaving a message on Sharon's voice mail.

AGNES: (*on phone*) Hey Sharon, it's Angie. I'm leaving a message in the back way 'cause it's pretty late. Just wanted to check in. Things are going really well. I'm looking into some meetings and um ... Things are ... Going really well. And I'm ... Feeling good. I'm feeling really good. Anyway. Take care.

AGNES hangs up and sits silently feeling neither "really good" nor that things are going "really well."

INT. CHRISSY'S CRAFT SHOP—DAY

JOANIE sits behind the counter bored beyond belief and picking at her fluorescent fingernail polish as she reads a barely thumbed paperback. We pan the aisles of various local crafts, much pottery and a few pieces of folk art. We find AGNES trying not to be conspicuous as she eyes JOANIE over a display of flat, wooden, hand-painted Christmas tree ornaments. JOANIE notices AGNES's strange behavior. After a moment:

JOANIE: Can I help you?

AGNES: Ah no ah yes, I was just looking for ...

AGNES grabs anything nearby, the ornament.

AGNES: ... another one of these.

JOANIE: There's none left there?

AGNES: Oh yes right sure there are, right here, yes, I see them.

AGNES grabs another ornament and heads for the counter.

AGNES: These, just, these two are, uh huh, good.

JOANIE begins to wrap them. AGNES watches her carefully, her hands, her face.

JOANIE: You're early for Christmas.

AGNES: Pardon me?

JOANIE: They're Christmas tree ornaments, you knew that right?

AGNES: Oh yeah, I like to be, early, for Christmas. But everything's … There are so many … You've got a lot of lovely things here in the store.

JOANIE: Some people like it.

AGNES notices some straw and feather dream-catchers on display at the cash register.

AGNES: These are those "dream-catchers" aren't they?

JOANIE: Uh huh.

AGNES: Do they work?

JOANIE: (*rolling her eyes*) Yeah they work. (*ringing in AGNES's purchase*) Twenty-five-seventy-six.

AGNES: I'm just visiting the area. I used to be from here. But now I'm just visiting. (*noting JOANIE's book*) What are you reading?

JOANIE: Some dumb book for school.

AGNES: (*reading the title*) Oh! *Jane Eyre.*

JOANIE: Did you read it?

AGNES: Oh yeah.

JOANIE: How does it end?

AGNES: Don't you want to get to the end yourself?

JOANIE: Not really.

AGNES: You should probably read it and find out for yourself.

JOANIE: (*flatly*) Thanks. Twenty-five-seventy-six.

AGNES hands over some bills.

AGNES: It's been a long time since I read it.

JOANIE gives AGNES her change.

JOANIE: Four-twenty-four is your change thank you have a nice day.

JOANIE sinks back into her book.

AGNES: Yes okay sure, have a nice day.

AGNES heads for the door. She stops.

AGNES: It's sad.

JOANIE: What is?

AGNES: *Jane Eyre*. The ending.

JOANIE: (*unimpressed*) Thanks.

AGNES: Sure.

AGNES leaves.

INT. KITCHEN/LIVING ROOM—EVENING

From the kitchen window we see THERESA's P.O.V. as she watches AGNES pull into the driveway. She quickly sits at the table and pretends to be reading the newspaper. LOUISE sits in the living room surfing television. AGNES enters with a small bag of groceries which she begins to put away.

AGNES: How's Mother doing?

THERESA: Sleeping a lot today.

AGNES: That's good.

THERESA: Where were you?

AGNES: Oh just cruising around.

LOUISE enters the kitchen and opens the fridge looking for a cola.

AGNES: Louise? Do you have any plans tomorrow night?

THERESA: (*laughing*) Plans. Yeah right.

LOUISE: (*to THERESA; irked*) I might.

THERESA: (*to LOUISE; laughing*) Get your date book out dear and see what your plans are.

LOUISE: Shut up.

AGNES: (*to LOUISE*) What if we had your friend over for dinner?

LOUISE: What friend?

AGNES: With the truck.

LOUISE: Dory?

THERESA: Louise doesn't want to be bothered with that sort of thing.

AGNES: Why not?

LOUISE: (*quickly jumping at the chance to bug THERESA*) Yeah let's have her over.

THERESA is bugged.

THERESA: You're going to have a party here with Mother upstairs sick?

AGNES: Not a party, just dinner.

THERESA: We don't have dinner anyways we have supper.

LOUISE: And maybe we could rent a video.

AGNES: We could rent a video.

THERESA: What video?

LOUISE: That TV show from England with the tall fella. You can get three or four of them on a tape. He's hilarious.

THERESA: I can't stand him.

LOUISE: Then you don't have to watch him.

LOUISE takes her cola and leaves the kitchen. THERESA shoots AGNES a steely gaze.

AGNES: (*to THERESA*) What?

THERESA: (*looking away*) What? Nothing.

THERESA returns to her newspaper and AGNES to her groceries. The women are silent. We hear:

DORY: (*v.o.*) Of Venezuela: Our Lady of Coromoto. Of Wales: Saint David. Of weavers: Saint Parasceva.

INT. ROSE'S BEDROOM—EARLY EVENING

The next evening. DORY's face fills the screen.

DORY: Of the West Indies: Saint Gertrude. Of widows: Saint Paula. Of winegrowers: Saint Vincent of Saragossa. Of writers: Saint Francis de Sales. Of young girls: Saint Agnes. Of youth: Saint Gabriel of the Sorrowful Mother.

DORY, AGNES and LOUISE stand around ROSE in her bed as she nurses a shot of rye. THERESA stands in the doorway. As DORY finishes the women applaud. ROSE's voice has grown weak and hoarse.

ROSE: Isn't that great!

DORY: Took me two years to get them all. I'm not perfect yet though. I think I missed one. Did I leave out Gabriel the Archangel? He's the one for postal workers.

THERESA: No I think you got them all.

DORY: There's a lot of them.

THERESA: There certainly is.

ROSE: Do you have any other talents dear?

DORY: I play a bit of guitar.

AGNES: Louise you used to play the guitar.

LOUISE: No I didn't.

ROSE: Where is that old guitar?

LOUISE: I don't know.

ROSE: Louise was good on the guitar.

LOUISE: (*quietly; embarrassed*) Shut up.

AGNES: I think the casserole's probably ready. Will I bring you up something Mother?

ROSE: (*indicating secretly to AGNES she wants her drink topped off*) No I'm fine dear.

The women move to exit. The telephone rings. THERESA dashes out ahead to get it.

THERESA: I'll get it, I'll get it.

INT. KITCHEN—EARLY EVENING

DORY, LOUISE and AGNES sit at the kitchen table, a cooling casserole as a centrepiece. The ubiquitous television drones on in the background. A silence at the table as the women wait for THERESA.

DORY: This looks just gorgeous. And salad, that's a treat.

AGNES: Louise maybe you'd like to go turn off the TV.

LOUISE: How come?

AGNES: Nobody's watching it. And we have company.

DORY: Oh no it's fine. It's nice on in the background.

THERESA rushes through the kitchen putting on her coat.

THERESA: Sorry everybody I gotta go. You go ahead without me. I'm taking the car Louise.

AGNES: Where are you going?

THERESA: I just have to go out for a little while.

THERESA leaves. AGNES rises and follows after her.

AGNES: Excuse me.

EXT. HOUSE—EVENING

AGNES follows after THERESA as she rushes down the driveway toward the car. DORY's red truck is on the street in front of the house.

AGNES: Where are you going?

THERESA: Donnie needs to see me. I'll be back in a little while.

AGNES takes THERESA's arm.

AGNES: Don't.

THERESA: Let me go.

AGNES: Wait now.

THERESA: (*getting into the car*) I'll be right back.

AGNES watches THERESA back down the driveway and off.

INT. HOUSE—EVENING

Later. AGNES, DORY and LOUISE sit at the table finishing up the casserole. LOUISE stares down at her plate shy to the point of speechlessness. AGNES and DORY try to keep a conversation going.

DORY: Well that was an excellent casserole. I'd ask you for the recipe but I'm not so much of a cook. Are you Louise?

LOUISE: What?

DORY: Are you much of a cook?

LOUISE: No.

AGNES: She makes the turkey at Christmas.

LOUISE: Once.

AGNES: But it was good.

LOUISE: No it wasn't.

AGNES: Anyway. Should we move into the living room? There's ice cream.

LOUISE: I'm pretty tired, thanks for supper. (*to DORY*) I'll see you later.

LOUISE leaves the room. AGNES and DORY smile nervously at one another.

EXT. HOUSE—NIGHT

Later. AGNES sits on the front step of the house reading Jane Eyre. *DORY's truck is gone. THERESA pulls into the driveway in the car. She gets out and sits beside AGNES on the step. Neither says anything for some time.*

AGNES: There's casserole left.

THERESA: I'm not really hungry. Thanks.

THERESA leans back on the step. After a moment:

THERESA: She left. Donnie. The girlfriend.

AGNES: What does he want you to do about it?

THERESA: He's upset.

AGNES: Serves him right.

THERESA sits quietly for a moment, then suddenly:

THERESA: It's all my fault anyway really. This whole mess. He wanted kids but I wouldn't. That's a sin for me.

AGNES: No it isn't.

THERESA: Say what you like Agnes, but it is.

AGNES: (*going back to the book*) Whatever.

THERESA waits for AGNES to continue the argument, but AGNES continues to read. THERESA lets it drop.

THERESA: (*re: book*) What's that?

AGNES: (*holding up the book*) Jane Eyre.

THERESA: (*taking the book from AGNES and thumbing through it lovingly*) Aww. I love that ending.

AGNES looks at THERESA and sees the romantic young girl she once was.

AGNES: There's ice cream.

INT. KITCHEN/LIVING ROOM—NIGHT

AGNES and THERESA sit watching the video LOUISE has rented and eating ice cream. A British sitcom with a laugh track. AGNES sprawls on the sofa and THERESA sits in LOUISE's chair. They laugh together along with the laugh track. LOUISE enters the kitchen. THERESA gets out of LOUISE's chair and bats AGNES's legs off the sofa so she can sit there.

AGNES: I thought you went to bed.

LOUISE: Where's the ice cream?

THERESA: In the fridge.

LOUISE: It'll get all soft.

THERESA: I like it soft.

LOUISE: Well I don't.

THERESA: Oh don't worry you'll eat it.

LOUISE enters with a bowl of ice cream and sits in her chair. The three sisters watch the video. They laugh together with the laugh track. We see them together for a moment as somehow, inexplicably alike. There is both a sadness and a comfort in this.

LOUISE: (*casually to* THERESA) Too bad you missed supper, it was fun.

AGNES: (*clearly stumped*) You didn't even stay for ice cream.

LOUISE: I'm having it now. (*a beat*) Where is that old guitar anyway?

THERESA: That got thrown out years ago.

AGNES: No I saw it in the basement.

LOUISE: I'm going to dig that up.

THERESA: Don't be starting with that racket.

AGNES: It'd be nice.

THERESA: Nice, yeah if you like a cat clawing on a blackboard.

LOUISE: Shut up, I will if I want to.

THERESA: (*to* LOUISE) Will you?

AGNES: (*to* THERESA) Leave her be.

LOUISE: (*to* THERESA) Yeah I will.

Suddenly they are separate, each gripped in her own thought. The laugh track blares on the video, the sisters do not laugh.

EXT. BACKYARD—DAY

The next day. LOUISE sits in a lawn chair working her fingers around a chord on the neck of an old acoustic guitar. DORY's hand comes into frame, guiding her fingers to the right position. LOUISE strums, the chord is clear and smooth. DORY, with her own guitar, sits close to LOUISE in a lawn chair.

INT. KITCHEN—DAY

AGNES stands in the window smoking, watching LOUISE and DORY. THERESA enters the kitchen with a bag of groceries.

THERESA: What's Dory's truck doing out there?

AGNES: (*stepping away from the window*) She's out back with Louise.

THERESA goes to the window and looks out.

EXT. BACKYARD—DAY

LOUISE and DORY play guitars quietly together. EVIE MACLELLAN appears in her adjoining backyard pretending to check her plants.

INT. KITCHEN—DAY

The sight of EVIE snooping is too much for THERESA. She calls out the window.

THERESA: (*out the window*) Louise! I'm about to get supper on now.

DORY: (*calling to THERESA*) How you doing Miss?

THERESA: (*out the window*) Fine Dory thanks, see you later. (*to AGNES*) You're responsible for this.

THERESA hurriedly goes about emptying potatoes and carrots from the grocery bag and starting supper.

AGNES: For what?

THERESA: Oh don't play all innocent with me.

AGNES: (*innocently*) What do you mean?

THERESA: Give me a hand here. (*re: potatoes*) Peel these. I'm just going to get supper on then I gotta go.

AGNES: Where?

THERESA: Donnie's. The place is in a terrible need of a clean. That one, I swear to God, she wouldn't lift her finger if the Pope was coming. (*indicating*) The dust is like this.

AGNES: So when are you moving back in?

THERESA: I'm going to clean the house, I'm not moving back in. Smarten up.

LOUISE sticks her head in the kitchen door.

LOUISE: I'm going up to Dory's to jam with her cousin, she's a drummer.

THERESA: What about supper?

LOUISE: We'll get something there. See ya.

LOUISE is gone. THERESA looks at AGNES.

AGNES: (*innocently*) What?

THERESA: (*angrily chopping a carrot*) "What?" "What?" indeed. "What?"

AGNES suppresses a smile.

INT. ROSE'S BEDROOM—NIGHT

ROSE's night table is filled with pill bottles, paperbacks and a small struggling African Violet. An opened bottle of rye sits incongruously amid the medicines. ROSE lies in bed, listening as AGNES reads Jane Eyre *to her, a slight smile on her face, her eyes half open, an empty glass clasped loosely in her hand. AGNES sits by the bed, in a chair near the window.*

AGNES: (*reading*) "Reader, though I look comfortable accommodated, I am not very tranquil in my mind. It is a very strange sensation to inexperienced youth to feel itself quite alone in the world, cut adrift from every connection, uncertain whether the port to which it is bound can be reached, and prevented by many impediments from returning to that it has quitted. The charm of adventure sweetens that sensation, the glow of pride warms it; but then the throb of fear disturbs it; and fear with me became predominant when time elapsed and I was still alone."

ROSE: (*not really hearing; almost a whisper*) That's nice.

EXT. CRAFT SHOP—DAY

AGNES sits in the parked sedan, a hundred metres down the road from its usual spot across from the craft shop.

INT. CAR—DAY

AGNES keeps her eyes on the door of the shop, She doesn't notice JOANIE suddenly appear from behind her. JOANIE knocks on AGNES's window. AGNES jumps a mile. She rolls down her window.

JOANIE: Hey.

AGNES: Oh. Hey. Hi.

JOANIE takes out a package of cigarettes, she takes one for herself and offers one to AGNES.

JOANIE: Smoke?

AGNES: No thank you.

JOANIE: I thought you weren't from around here.

AGNES: I'm not. I mean I am. From Sydney. I don't live there anymore though. I mean I haven't lived there in a while.

JOANIE: Where do you live?

AGNES: Toronto.

JOANIE: Oh yeah.

AGNES: Yeah.

JOANIE: What's Toronto like?

AGNES: Good, nice, parts of it.

JOANIE: I heard it sucks.

AGNES: Sort of, sometimes, can.

JOANIE: Probably not as much as this place sucks though. So what are you doing sitting out here?

AGNES: Just waiting to … go. Which, actually I probably better do.

JOANIE: Whatever.

AGNES: See you later now.

JOANIE: Whatever.

AGNES rolls up her window and drives away. JOANIE watches after her.

EXT. HOUSE—DAY

AGNES pulls around the corner heading home when she sees an ambulance parked in front of the house. She pulls into the driveway and dashes out leaving the door open behind her.

INT. KITCHEN—DAY

AGNES dashes into the kitchen just as TWO PARAMEDICS are leaving. LOUISE sits at the table.

AGNES: What's going on?

LOUISE: There was nobody here.

AGNES: What happened?

THERESA enters the kitchen.

THERESA: (*sternly*) She's fine now.

AGNES: What happened?

THERESA: I got home and she wasn't breathing right and then she started choking so I called the doctor. Then the doctor called the ambulance.

AGNES: What was it?

THERESA: The tumors are all into her larynx.

AGNES: Oh God.

THERESA: They've got her on oxygen. Apparently her voice is pretty much gone.

AGNES: (*to LOUISE*) You said you were going to be here.

LOUISE: You said you were going to be home at three o'clock.

AGNES: I didn't say that. Where were you?

THERESA: (*to AGNES*) She was off running the roads with Dory. Where were you?

AGNES: Nowhere I was …

THERESA: Cruising around?

THERESA goes outside leaving AGNES and LOUISE alone.

LOUISE: You said you were going to be home—

AGNES: Shut up.

INT. ROSE'S BEDROOM—EVENING

A little while later. Early evening. ROSE sits up in bed as best she can, there is an oxygen tank and mask beside the bed. AGNES steps into the doorway. When ROSE speaks it's clear her voice is failing. She is much more frail than we have seen her. After a moment:

AGNES: How are you?

ROSE: Where's Theresa?

AGNES: I think she's out back.

ROSE: Well hurry up and give me a cigarette.

AGNES: I don't think—

ROSE: I'm not interested in your thinking I want your cigarettes.

AGNES takes out a cigarette and lights it.

ROSE: Where you been spending all your time these days? Hm?

AGNES gives the cigarette to her mother.

AGNES: Just … on my own.

ROSE: On your own.

AGNES: Uh huh.

ROSE: That's not like you.

AGNES: I'm not so much like me as I used to be.

ROSE smiles. She takes a drag of her cigarette. She begins to cough, AGNES comes to her aid. She sits ROSE up in bed and rubs her back as ROSE continues to cough. ROSE struggles to speak to her daughter.

ROSE: (*faintly*) You do what you have to do.

AGNES: What?

ROSE: (*more clearly*) You do what you have to do.

AGNES: (*still coughing; touching AGNES's face*) You do what you have to do.

ROSE's coughing gets worse. THERESA rushes into the room.

THERESA: Mother? (*to AGNES*) She needs to take some oxygen. (*noticing the cigarette in ROSE's hand*) For God's sake … (*to AGNES*) Did you give her this?

THERESA takes the cigarette from ROSE.

THERESA: (*to AGNES*) What are you nuts?

AGNES: I'm sorry.

THERESA: (*handing the cigarette to AGNES*) Go on, take this, go on get out of here with this.

AGNES takes the cigarette and leaves. THERESA helps ROSE on with the oxygen mask.

INT. KITCHEN—EVENING

Later. AGNES sits at the kitchen table. THERESA comes downstairs after settling ROSE in to sleep. THERESA puts the kettle on for tea. We hear the television from the living room where LOUISE watches it.

THERESA: You can't be letting her smoke Agnes.

AGNES: Theresa?

THERESA: I got her some of that nicotine gum.

AGNES: Theresa?

THERESA: You can give her a piece of that if she's having a nic fit.

AGNES: Theresa?

THERESA: What?

AGNES: I think we should go see Dad.

THERESA: Stop it.

AGNES: I think we should.

> LOUISE *steps in from the living room.*

LOUISE: What?

AGNES: I think we should go see Dad.

LOUISE: Why?

THERESA: Absolutely not. We're not getting into that. Not while Mother's alive that's for sure.

AGNES: I think it's the right thing to do.

THERESA: What do you know about the right thing to do?

> THERESA *opens a cupboard above the refrigerator and takes out a small paper bag. She drops it on the table in front of* AGNES.

THERESA: Is this the right thing to do?

AGNES: What?

THERESA: Where did you get these?

> THERESA *takes the two flat wooden Christmas ornaments out of the bag and drops them on the table.*

AGNES: I saw them at a—

THERESA: You going to lie to me? The name of the store's on the price tag.

> AGNES *says nothing.*

THERESA: You promised me you weren't going to start anything.

AGNES: I'm not starting anything.

THERESA: So you talked to her? Did you talk to her?

AGNES: Yes.

LOUISE: You saw her?

THERESA: Does she know who you are?

AGNES: No.

THERESA: She better not. Do you hear me?

AGNES: Or what?

THERESA: Or maybe you should start thinking about making your way back home.

AGNES: I'm just trying to make sense of some things.

THERESA: What you should do— (*to LOUISE*) And you too. Both of you— (*to LOUISE*) You stop it with this Dory thing— (*to AGNES*)And you stop it with your "cruising around." Both of you, what you need to do is get your shit together, and think about what's going on right here in this house. You hear me!

THERESA noisily makes tea. LOUISE skulks back to the television. AGNES sits silently at the table, feeling like a little girl again.

INT. LIVING ROOM—DAY

A couple of days later. LOUISE sits in the living room half-heartedly picking out a chord progression on the guitar.

INT. KITCHEN—DAY

AGNES has cleaned house again. She wears rubber gloves and frantically works at an old stain on the counter near the stove. In the living room LOUISE continues to explore the same chord progression over and over. The guitar wears quickly on AGNES. She tries to ignore it but her nerves get the best of her.

AGNES: Louise for God's sake.

LOUISE: What?

AGNES: Would you stop with that, watch television or something.

LOUISE: There's nothing on.

AGNES: Then go see Mother.

LOUISE: She's sleeping.

AGNES: (*at the end of her patience*) Then go watch her sleep.

Not wanting to argue LOUISE takes the guitar and goes upstairs. AGNES pulls off the gloves and throws them on the counter.

INT. BATHROOM—DAY

Later. AGNES finishes her makeup and hair. She looks put together in a way we haven't seen before. We can hear LOUISE quietly playing guitar in ROSE's room. AGNES leaves the bathroom.

INT. ROSE'S BEDROOM—DAY

LOUISE sits by ROSE's bed playing a sad tune on the guitar. ROSE is awake listening. AGNES appears in the doorway. She watches a moment until LOUISE looks up and sees her. LOUISE stops playing.

AGNES: I've got to run out for a little while.

LOUISE: See ya.

LOUISE goes back to playing. ROSE picks up a notepad and pencil from her night table. This is how she communicates now for the most part. She writes a note and hands it to AGNES. AGNES steps into the room and takes it. She looks at the note then shoves it quickly into her pocket.

AGNES: (*quickly departing*) You too. Bye bye.

EXT. CHRISSY'S CRAFT SHOP—LATE AFTERNOON

The sedan sits outside the shop.

INT. CAR—LATE AFTERNOON

AGNES sits in the sedan outside the craft shop. She wears large dark glasses and smokes a cigarette. She seems both relaxed and agitated at the same time. She lifts a small bottle in a paper bag to her lips and drinks in a long gulp.

INT. CHRISSY'S CRAFT SHOP—LATE AFTERNOON

A ceramic bell ringing. AGNES holds a small hand bell which she is purchasing from JOANIE at the cash register. AGNES is not drunk yet, but certainly looser. JOANIE notices something different about her. AGNES smiles a broad smile behind her big sunglasses.

AGNES: It's so pretty. And handy. If you wanted to get some-one's attention. You wouldn't have to yell. Just … (*She rings the bell.*)

With a flourish AGNES drops the bell in her bag.

JOANIE: I like your glasses.

AGNES takes off her glasses. She offers them to JOANIE.

AGNES: Here try them on.

JOANIE finds this odd.

JOANIE: Uh. No thanks.

AGNES puts them on the counter.

AGNES: Have them.

JOANIE: No that's okay.

AGNES: I've got pairs coming out of my ears.

JOANIE leaves the sunglasses where AGNES put them. AGNES takes JOANIE's hand in hers.

AGNES: Look at your nails, what a pretty colour.

JOANIE: (*taking her hand away*) They're all chipped.

AGNES: You got a pen?

JOANIE hands her a pen. AGNES grabs some paper from the counter.

AGNES: If you ever get stuck in Sydney and you need a place to stay. Here.

AGNES hands the paper to JOANIE.

JOANIE: What is it?

AGNES: That's me. We've got lots of room. If you're ever stuck for a place I mean.

AGNES wanders around the store. She stops to admire a landscape painting by the door.

JOANIE: It's a bit of a drive for you every day isn't it, from Sydney to here.

AGNES: Not too bad. It's pleasant.

JOANIE: What's pleasant about it?

AGNES: Oh you know, the scenery. Like this. (*She indicates the painting she admires.*) This is beautiful.

JOANIE: My mother did that. That's where most of this crap comes from. You want to talk to her? (*calling into the back room*) Chrissy!

AGNES immediately loses her nerve.

AGNES: Oh um no no that's fine no.

AGNES moves quickly out the door.

CHRISSY: (*o.c.*) What is it dear?

AGNES: (*nervously calling back to CHRISSY*) Nothing! (*leaving*) I've got to go, but tell … tell her … Nothing. Bye

AGNES leaves. JOANIE watches out the window as AGNES dashes across the street. CHRISSY, late 40s, a former hippy, enters from the back. JOANIE picks up the sunglasses from the counter and tucks them under her arm.

CHRISSY: Who was that?

JOANIE: Some freak.

CHRISSY: (*mildly scolding*) Joanie.

JOANIE: Well she was.

JOANIE lights a cigarette.

CHRISSY: Cigarettes outside please.

CHRISSY looks out the window.

EXT. CHRISSY'S CRAFT SHOP—LATE AFTERNOON

AGNES hurries into the sedan and pulls away.

INT. CHRISSY'S CRAFT SHOP—LATE AFTERNOON

CHRISSY watches after AGNES. AGNES looks vaguely familiar to her.

JOANIE: (*o.c.*) (*mocking*) "Cigarettes outside please."

EXT. HOTEL PARKING LOT—NIGHT

Later. A lovely night. The sedan sits in a hotel parking lot which runs along the harbour. A couple of small pleasure craft move slowly across the still surface of the water.

INT. CAR—NIGHT

AGNES sits in the car. She fumbles with the lid on her bottle and begins to drink it down in large greedy gulps. She winces against the sharpness of it, regroups, then goes for more. This time it's too much, she quickly opens the door and vomits. She pulls herself back into the car, takes a breath and goes back to the bottle. This time she manages to keep it down. She puts the cover back on the bottle and fixes her lipstick in the rearview mirror.

INT. HOTEL BAR—NIGHT

AGNES sits on a stool at the hotel bar. A fresh second (or third) drink appears for her. The BARTENDER indicates a BUSINESSMAN at the end of the bar. AGNES looks down the bar at him. He is late 40s, slightly out of shape but still attractive. He nods at her. She smiles flirtatiously as she looks away. Finally he speaks.

BUSINESSMAN: How are you doing?

AGNES looks at him.

AGNES: How are you doing?

BUSINESSMAN: Getting better.

AGNES: That seems to be going around.

AGNES smiles and takes a long drink.

INT. HOTEL ROOM—NIGHT

We see the end of the BUSINESSMAN's bed, his naked legs hanging face down off the edge. AGNES steps into frame buttoning her shirt.

BUSINESSMAN: Hey? Where you going?

AGNES: I don't know but I'm in a hurry to get there.

AGNES bumps into the wall as she grabs her bag and jacket and heads out the door.

INT. TAVERN—NIGHT

The wood-panelled tavern near the end of the night. The juke box bleats a schmaltzy waltz as TWO COUPLES grope on the tiny dance floor. The BARTENDER is tending to his last remaining customers at the bar: A COUPLE OF REGULARS, each alone, hunched over their drinks. At a table in the middle of the room sits AGNES with MARLENE, SANDY and a young tattooed, wild-haired man of 25, MICKEY. Two full pitchers of beer sit on the table. SANDY is slumped over with his chin on his chest. MARLENE vies for MICKEY's attention while AGNES now quite drunk holds him enthralled.

AGNES: The problem is you see, the problem is we turn it into a problem. That's the thing right. The problem is they've got everybody saying "Oh I've got a problem, Oh I've got a problem," right—so of course they've got a problem because they've got them saying they do.

MARLENE: Yeah well I—

AGNES: And there's some poor sap you know: "Joe's been sober for nineteen years on Tuesday," and they're all clapping and there's poor Joe white-knuckling it at one end of the table, looking about as dried out and fucked up, and you can see all the guy needs is a drink.

MICKEY: Just have a good time.

MARLENE: Yeah I know one time I—

AGNES: Basically it's just a dating service for neurotics.

MARLENE: Yeah, my—

AGNES: Who needs that! And everybody's got to tell their goddamn story. I'm sick of telling my goddamn story. That's why I come down here see, where nobody wants to talk about it. It's all "Shhhhh." That's what they should put on the sign over the goddamn causeway as you drive onto the island, instead of "A Hundred Thousand Welcomes" or whatever it is. Just put "Shhhhh."

AGNES rises from the table and speaks to the room.

AGNES: Does anybody want to hear my story?

MARLENE: (*embarrassed*) Agnes sit down.

AGNES: Ah shut up Marlene you're drunk.

MICKEY laughs.

AGNES: Nobody wants to hear my story? Okay then does anybody want to dance?

MICKEY: I'll dance with you.

AGNES grabs him and drags him onto the dance floor.

AGNES: You bet you will.

INT. TAVERN—NIGHT

Later. Hard rock on the jukebox. The place has cleared out but for our foursome. SANDY stands weavingly at the bar speaking to the bartender.

SANDY: Can I just get one to go?

BARTENDER: No Sandy, go home.

SANDY weaves away. The BARTENDER steps out from behind the bar. On the dance floor AGNES and MICKEY waltz to the fast song. Actually it's less waltzing than necking. The BARTENDER appears and unplugs the jukebox.

BARTENDER: All right ladies and gentlemen drink up now, time to head out.

The lack of music does not disrupt AGNES and MICKEY's neckfest. MARLENE appears with coats and bags.

MARLENE: We gotta go you guys.

AGNES: Where are we going?

MARLENE: I don't know. (*to MICKEY*) You wanna go for coffee?

AGNES: Coffee come on! Where's the party?

MICKEY: I'm the party.

AGNES and MICKEY wander off followed by MARLENE.

MARLENE: All right, I'm up for a party.

INT. BASEMENT APARTMENT—NIGHT

A small dirty one-room basement apartment. Boxes and boxes of crap. A skinny, frizzy-haired woman, SUE, 25, sits watching curling on television while MICKEY cuts lines of bad coke on a small mirror. AGNES sits on a rickety kitchen chair drinking a can of beer. MARLENE stands by the door holding her can of beer like a security blanket.

AGNES: Now this is me right? This is the me I am. No apologies that's it. All that other stuff of me that's just me trying not to be me. Life is hard and you've got to find whatever little ways out you can.

MICKEY: Tomorrow morning's going to be shit so let's have fun tonight.

MICKEY does a line off the mirror.

AGNES: Egg-fucking-zactly!

MARLENE: (*checking her watch*) It's already tomorrow morning.

MICKEY hands the mirror to MARLENE.

MARLENE: You've got to be kidding. I'm going Agnes are you coming?

MICKEY hands the mirror to AGNES.

AGNES: (*to MARLENE*) You've got to be kidding.

AGNES takes the mirror and does a line. MARLENE leaves.

MARLENE: See ya around.

AGNES: Right on.

INT. BASEMENT APARTMENT—DAWN

Later. The television plays early morning cartoons. MICKEY, now bare-chested, sits doing bicep curls with a ten-pound barbell. SUE and AGNES sit at a small kitchen table. AGNES confides her story to SUE as SUE uses her finger to lick the remaining coke residue from the mirror.

AGNES: So what am I going to do right? I mean what do I know. I mean but I know what's going on right. I'm fifteen. I don't have to be told. It's my body I know what's going on with it. So I know.

SUE: And it was your dad?

AGNES: Yeah.

SUE: Like your step-dad or your dad dad?

AGNES: My father.

SUE: Wow that could make a book.

AGNES: Yeah I could write a fucking book.

SUE: So what happened?

AGNES: So I knew. No one had to tell me I just knew. And so I tell my sisters, and we kind of turn it into a … We all get excited because we think: It'll be great, right? I'll have it and it'll be a little baby for all of us to love and to love us. And maybe we'd even be able to keep it a secret or something. I mean it had all been a secret already for so long so why not.

AGNES drifts off for a moment.

AGNES: And we so so wanted her to be a girl. Because then we'd be this perfect kind of family of these four kind of perfect sisters. We were going to call her Marion Bridge, like after the song. You know, (*singing*) "I'll trade you ten of your cities for Marion Bridge and the pleasure she brings."

SUE: Oh I love that song. We got that tape.

AGNES: If we could just have Marion Bridge there'd be ... everything would change.

AGNES drifts off again.

SUE: (*singing*) "Out on the Mira we ... " How's the rest of it go? (*to MICKEY*) Where's that tape? Mickey? Where's that tape we got off that band in Bras d'Or last summer? It got that "Out on the Mira" on it.

AGNES picks up the mirror from the table and looks at herself. SUE and MICKEY begin to bicker as AGNES continues to look at herself.

SUE: Mickey? Where's that tape at?

MICKEY: I don't know. Gimmie that line now.

SUE: What line now? There's no lines.

MICKEY: Fuck you! There was three on the mirror!

SUE: There was one for me and one for her and that's it!

MICKEY: Fucking not there was three!

AGNES catches a bit of daylight in the mirror. She looks up to a small basement window. She goes to the window and looks out. AGNES's P.O.V. out the window, down the sidewalk to the industrial waterfront. We stay on this P.O.V. while SUE and MICKEY bicker away.

SUE: (*o.c.*) I'm not lyin' Mickey!

MICKEY: (*o.c.*) I was saving that!

SUE: (*o.c.*) Well it's gone. Find me that tape, where's that tape?

MICKEY: (*o.c.*) I was saving that, Jesus Christ!

SUE: (*o.c.*) I wanna play that song, I gotta hear that song.

AGNES appears outside, unsteadily heading down the sidewalk toward the waterfront.

EXT. HOTEL PARKING LOT—DAWN

Close on the shore line. We move up toward the parking lot and find AGNES sitting on the rocky shore. She reaches into her pocket for a cigarette and finds ROSE's note. She looks at it. We see that ROSE has drawn a heart. AGNES tries to cry but cannot. She gets up and walks to the car which sits in the lot behind her. She gets in and drives away.

EXT. HOUSE—MORNING

AGNES pulls the car into the driveway. She gets up and walks into the backyard. THERESA appears in her house-coat standing in the doorway of the house.

INT. BACKYARD—DAY

AGNES is sitting in a lawn chair. THERESA approaches AGNES, her housecoat pulled around her against the morning chill.

THERESA: (*gently*) So is this the go again?

AGNES shakes her head "no."

THERESA: I was up all night. I couldn't sleep. I was worried about you. I feel like … I don't know … Just … Sometimes I'm such a cow, I don't know why.

AGNES looks at THERESA.

THERESA: Is it my fault?

AGNES: No.

AGNES is about to cry.

THERESA: Agnes please don't, Agnes don't. Please.

AGNES: Why not?

THERESA: 'Cause if you start I'll start and if I start I might not stop.

AGNES gets it together.

THERESA: You okay?

AGNES nods her head "yes."

THERESA: Do you want a cup of tea?

AGNES starts to cry.

THERESA: (*crying*) Oh Agnes …

AGNES: (*crying*) I'll have a cup of tea.

THERESA: (*crying*) Come on.

AGNES stands, THERESA puts her arm around her shoulders and walks with her toward the house.

EXT. HOUSE—DAY

THERESA and AGNES walk together toward the house. EVIE MACLELLAN peeks from behind her curtain next door. Without looking at her THERESA stops.

THERESA: (*to AGNES*) Hang on a sec.

THERESA bends down and in one motion picks up a clump of dirt and throws it at EVIE's house. EVIE darts away. THERESA bends down and picks up another, she hands it to AGNES. AGNES has a throw at the house.

WIDE ON: the two sisters, like mischievous girls, bombard the neighbour's house with dirt balls.

INT. ROSE'S BEDROOM—DAY

The next day. The bell AGNES purchased at the craft shop rings. ROSE sits up in bed, a notepad in her lap. She rings the bell again noisily.

EXT. HOUSE—DAY

LOUISE washes down the side of EVIE's house with a garden hose. THERESA appears in the doorway.

THERESA: Louise, leave that a minute Mother wants to see us.

LOUISE drops the hose and heads into the house.

LOUISE: I never made the mess why do I have to clean it up?

THERESA: Because you're the youngest.

LOUISE: Agnes is the youngest!

THERESA: Because you're the strongest.

LOUISE: (*flattered despite herself*) Whatever.

INT. ROSE'S BEDROOM—DAY

ROSE sits up in bed. She is very frail now and has great trouble breathing. AGNES is already in the room, in a chair by her mother's bed. THERESA and LOUISE enter.

THERESA: All right Mother we're here so, what?

ROSE takes a page from the notepad and hands it to AGNES. ROSE indicates that AGNES read the note. AGNES begins to read it silently. ROSE indicates that she should read it out loud.

AGNES: (*reading*) "My dear girls, I know there've been times I haven't been the mother I should have been. Times when I turned away from some things I didn't want to see." (*to ROSE*) Mother …

ROSE indicates that she should keep reading.

AGNES: (*reading*) "But at those times I always believed that I was doing what was best for everybody. And in the case of things that have gone on—"

THERESA: Mother don't now—

ROSE: (*with what's left of her voice; angry*) Shut up.

AGNES: "And in the case of things that have gone on, all we can do is look to see if there's beautiful things in the terrible things. From where I sit now, all I can do is see where I went wrong, look for the good in it, and hope, because of the good, for forgiveness."

AGNES looks at ROSE. ROSE hands AGNES a second piece of paper.

AGNES: (*reading*) "And while I'm waiting for forgiveness could we have a little fiddle and a bit of a drink?"

The girls laugh.

INT. HALLWAY—NIGHT

We look into ROSE's room where we see the remains of the women's party. ROSE lies in bed writing a note which she hands to THERESA who sits in the chair by the window, her feet up on the bed. A gentle fiddle drifts from the boom box.

THERESA: No Mother it's too late.

ROSE quickly writes another note and hands it to THERESA. THERESA reads it.

THERESA: Mother please, we'll all go outside one night when it's warmer.

ROSE writes another note and hands it to THERESA. THERESA pauses a moment before she takes it.

THERESA: Do I even have to look at this Mother?

ROSE continues to hold the note out to THERESA. THERESA takes it and reads it.

THERESA: I love you too Mother.

We DOLLY past the bathroom where AGNES is just turning off the light and follow her a few steps down the hallway until she enters the room she shares with LOUISE.

INT. LOUISE AND AGNES'S ROOM—NIGHT

AGNES enters the dark room and settles into bed. LOUISE is already in bed on the other side of the room. From the next room we can still hear THERESA.

THERESA: (*o.c.*) Another one? No Mother it's still too chilly out I said, another time. (*a beat*) You're going to wear that pencil out Mother. Yes Mother I love you too.

LOUISE and AGNES speak in hushed tones in the darkened room.

LOUISE: (*humorously*) Mother's big on the "love you" now that she doesn't have to say it.

AGNES: I think she just likes drawing hearts.

After a moment.

AGNES: What do you want Louise?

LOUISE: What do you mean?

AGNES: I mean generally.

LOUISE: To be, you mean? As a job like?

AGNES: Sure.

LOUISE: I don't know.

A silence then:

LOUISE: One thing I think of sometimes is …

AGNES: What?

LOUISE: Kind of, a mover.

AGNES: What kind of mover?

LOUISE: A mover. Like when you're going to move from one house to another one or one apartment to another one. Because most times people are moving to a nicer place, so it's probably a good feeling, to take somebody someplace better. And even if it's a worse place, if you're a mover, you can walk in and look around for the good stuff and tell the people, "Oh this window's nice," or "The floor's better," or "You didn't need a big yard anyway." So it'd be like you'd be helping people plus get to drive. I like driving.

AGNES: That sounds like a good idea.

LOUISE: I guess. (*a beat*) What do you want?

After a moment:

AGNES: I don't know.

INT. KITCHEN—DAY

The next morning. LOUISE and AGNES, neither the best first thing in the morning, struggle with making breakfast. THERESA enters and hovers nervously nearby, it's clear there's something on her mind. After a moment:

THERESA: (*to AGNES*) I was thinking about what Mother said about the good in the bad.

AGNES: Yes?

THERESA: Can we see her?

AGNES: Who?

THERESA: The girl.

AGNES: What girl?

THERESA: (*meaningfully*) The girl.

LOUISE: Joan?

AGNES: They call her Joanie.

THERESA: Can we see her?

AGNES: We can do that.

LOUISE: I don't want to see her.

THERESA: And we better do it now, otherwise I'll lose my nerve. I'll be in the car.

THERESA leaves.

EXT. TOWN MAIN STREET—DAY

The sedan sits a hundred metres down from the craft shop.

INT. CAR—DAY

AGNES sits behind the wheel. THERESA sits beside her. THERESA's nervousness is affecting AGNES. They have been waiting for some time.

THERESA: Are you drinking these days?

AGNES: No.

THERESA: I could use a shot.

AGNES: There she is.

AGNES toots the horn lightly.

EXT. CHRISSY'S CRAFT SHOP—DAY

WIDE AS: We watch as JOANIE sees and approaches the car. AGNES gets out and speaks to her for a moment. AGNES encourages THERESA to get out of the car. JOANIE indicates that they should follow her. They do.

INT. CHRISSY'S CRAFT SHOP—DAY

CHRISSY watches from the window of the craft shop as JOANIE leads AGNES and THERESA around the corner.

INT. APARTMENT—DAY

A sparsely furnished, dingy, two-room apartment above a bar. The place would make frat house decor look lush by comparison. Cardboard banana boxes for tables, a flowered flannel sheet as a curtain. A couple of touches (a scarf on a lamp, a hat hung on a wall) are probably JOANIE's. THERESA and AGNES sit on a tired old sofa. JOANIE rummages in the mostly empty fridge.

THERESA: (*to AGNES*) Five minutes and we're going.

JOANIE opens two beers and hands one to AGNES.

AGNES: Oh. No thanks.

THERESA: I'll take one.

JOANIE gives the beer to THERESA. THERESA drinks her beer nervously. JOANIE takes the other for herself.

THERESA: You're not old enough to drink.

JOANIE: What are you a cop?

THERESA: No.

JOANIE: Relax. (*to AGNES*) Sure you don't want one there's tons.

AGNES: No thanks, I'm driving.

JOANIE: Whatever. My boyfriend drives better when he's drinking. He can concentrate on the road better he says.

AGNES: This is your boyfriend's place?

JOANIE: Yeah Steve. What's your names?

THERESA: Carmel. She's Carmel and I'm …

AGNES: Camille.

JOANIE: Which one's which?

THERESA: (*pointing at AGNES*) Carmel.

AGNES: (*pointing at THERESA*) Camille.

JOANIE: I'm Joanie. Joanie sucks.

AGNES: It's nice.

JOANIE: It is not. It's not my real name anyway. I don't know my real name.

THERESA: Oh yeah? (*to AGNES*) We should probably get going.

JOANIE: Do you want another beer?

THERESA: Uh, oh no thanks. Uh Camille? Maybe we should get going?

JOANIE: (*to THERESA*) I thought you were Camille?

THERESA: Oh yeah, I am, I was just talking to myself. Carmel? Should we? Get going?

AGNES: Yes I guess, yes. Thanks for the beer.

JOANIE: You didn't have a beer.

THERESA: Thanks for mine. Bye now.

AGNES: Bye.

AGNES and THERESA leave. JOANIE watches them leave from the window.

EXT. TOWN MAIN STREET—DAY

THERESA leads AGNES to the car.

THERESA: She's too young to have a boyfriend.

AGNES: How old were you when you met Donnie?

THERESA: Oh shut up.

AGNES: "Carmel?"

THERESA: "Camille?!"

AGNES: It's better than "Carmel."

THERESA: She knows.

AGNES: She doesn't know.

THERESA: She knows.

INT. APARTMENT—DAY

JOANIE watches them leave from the window. She takes AGNES's sunglasses from her pocket and puts them on.

INT. ROSE'S BEDROOM—NIGHT

That night. ROSE lies in bed sleeping. THERESA sits by the window, lost in thought, listening as AGNES sits by the bed in the chair reading the end of Jane Eyre *to ROSE.*

AGNES: (*reading*) " … reverently lifting his hat from his brow, and bending his sightless eyes to the earth, he stood in mute devotion. Only the last words of his worship were audible—'I thank my Maker, that in the midst of judgment, He has remembered mercy.' Then he stretched his hand out to be led. I took that dear hand, held it a moment to my lips, and then let it pass round my shoulder: being so much lower of stature than he, I served both for his prop and his guide. We entered the wood, and wended homeward."

AGNES closes the book. THERESA holds out her hand to AGNES for the book. AGNES gives it to her. THERESA takes looks at the passage AGNES has just read. THERESA closes the book, after a moment she tosses it out the window and leaves the room.

AGNES: Theresa what … ?

AGNES rises and looks out the window. We hear THERESA descending the stairs.

AGNES: (*calling after her; quietly*) Where are you going?

The kitchen door shuts and the car starts. AGNES watches her mother breathing as we hear the car pull away from the house.

EXT. HOUSE—NIGHT

Later. AGNES sits on the front step smoking. The Jane Eyre *book beside her on the step. THERESA pulls the sedan into the driveway. She gets out and leans against the car. Nothing is said for a few moments.*

THERESA: Sorry about the book.

AGNES: I'm sure it's not the first time she's been thrown out a window.

Another silence and then:

THERESA: Donnie shaved off his moustache.

AGNES: When?

THERESA: Last year when all this craziness started. But just tonight, talking to him, it's like I never really noticed his mouth before. It's so ... soft or something. Soft like it's just there moving, moving away, not meaning anything. I was watching him and I thought, it's not like the kind of mouth you could trust anything it said. And then I thought, that's why I never gave him kids, I didn't trust him. And then I thought, I don't trust anybody. You know?

AGNES: I know.

THERESA: I guess that's something to work on. Once I get done with this.

THERESA moves to open the back door of the car.

AGNES: With what?

THERESA opens the door to reveal a small sapling in the backseat.

THERESA: Give me a hand with this tree.

EXT. BACKYARD—DAY

A week later. AGNES takes bright yellow and blue sheets down from the clothes line. She drops the sheets in a basket and walks back to the house, passing the sapling which is slowly beginning to bud planted smack in the middle of the barren backyard.

EXT. BACKYARD—AFTERNOON

Another week later. The sapling begins to thrive. Nearby THERESA plants a bed of pansies.

EXT. BACKYARD—NIGHT

The sapling glimmers in moonlight reflecting off the house. LOUISE passes with a gas lantern and a blanket. She places the lantern on a small table beside ROSE who sits wrapped in blankets in a lawn chair. LOUISE puts the blanket on ROSE's lap. AGNES and THERESA sit on either side of ROSE. LOUISE sits across from ROSE making a circle of four. We feel the other women but our focus is ROSE. Slowly she becomes incredibly alert as she looks up into the starry sky.

THERESA: You all right there Mother?

AGNES: Are her feet cold check her feet Louise.

LOUISE: (*checking*) She's all right, she's good.

THERESA: It's not too chilly is it?

AGNES: No, it's nice.

THERESA: Mother? Are you all right there Mother?

Slowly, in a tiny voice ROSE, looking up into the sky, begins to speak. It's not clear what she is saying.

AGNES: What Mother? Are you all right?

LOUISE: Is she saying something?

ROSE's voice becomes clearer.

ROSE: Star light, star bright … First star I see tonight …

ROSE holds her hand out to AGNES. AGNES takes ROSE's hand. THERESA takes ROSE's hand and holds out her hand to LOUISE. LOUISE takes AGNES's hand. The women hold hands in a circle. ROSE continues the rhyme as the world fills with stars.

ROSE: I wish I may ... I wish I might ... Have the wish ... I wish tonight ...

Quietly a guitar. A girl's voice singing in a sweet, faltering voice, a hymn called "Be Not Afraid."

GIRL: (*v.o.*) (*singing*) "You shall cross the barren desert, / but you shall not die of thirst. / You shall wander far in safety / though you do not know the way. / You shall speak your words to foreign men / and they will understand. / Know that I am with you through it all."

INT. CHURCH—DAY

We see the GIRL, 15, singing. Beside her LOUISE accompanies her on the guitar. We see the congregation at Rose's funeral: TWO DOZEN people including: EVIE MACLELLAN, SEVERAL PEOPLE from the prayer meeting, DORY, MARLENE and SANDY, finally THERESA and AGNES. The song continues.

GIRL: (*singing*) "Be not afraid. / I go before you always; / Come follow me, / and I will give you rest. / If you pass through raging waters / in the sea, you shall not drown. / If you walk amid the burning flames, / you shall not be harmed. / If you stand before the power of hell / and death is at your side, / know that I am with you through it all. / Be not afraid. / I go before you always; / Come follow me, / and I will give you rest."

EXT. HOUSE—DAY

A week later. In the backyard. AGNES and THERESA check on the health of the tree. The have just added fertilizer to the soil. They wipe their hands and survey their handiwork.

AGNES: I just worry that it's got no shade.

THERESA: It's a tree it's supposed to give shade.

AGNES: It's still a bit sad.

THERESA: So would you be if you'd been living under that killer for a year.

LOUISE comes around the edge of the house.

LOUISE: You guys?

THERESA: What?

LOUISE: There's somebody here to see you.

CHRISSY comes around the corner behind LOUISE.

CHRISSY: Hello.

AGNES: Oh.

THERESA: (*to AGNES*) Is that … ?

AGNES: Yeah.

THERESA: Oh.

LOUISE: (*to CHRISSY*) Hello.

INT. LIVING ROOM—DAY

CHRISSY, LOUISE and AGNES sit in the living room. THERESA stands nearby.

CHRISSY: So which one of you is Angie?

AGNES: I'm Agnes … Angie … Agnes …

CHRISSY: Of course.

THERESA: I'm Theresa. And this is Louise. Louise why don't you put the kettle on, maybe Mrs. …

CHRISSY: Chrissy.

THERESA: … maybe Chrissy would like a cup of tea.

CHRISSY: No I'm fine thank you. (*a moment*) I was sorry to hear about your mother.

THERESA: Thank you.

CHRISSY: So. Have you all been to see her or … ?

THERESA: No. Just ... I have ... And her. (*indicates AGNES*) Us. We have.

CHRISSY: And what have you told her?

AGNES: Nothing.

CHRISSY: And what are you planning on telling her?

AGNES: I don't ... know.

CHRISSY: When she asks about her father what will you say?

The sisters shift uncomfortably.

CHRISSY: (*to AGNES*) I'm sure it's a painful thing for you. I imagine for all of you. But Joanie ... She's a teenager, she's going through a difficult time. She's wonderful but ... She's a handful. Just think about how it might affect her.

AGNES: I don't want to cause any trouble.

CHRISSY: It would really help if you could tell me what you did want?

AGNES: I ... don't know.

CHRISSY rises.

CHRISSY: Joanie will be eighteen in a couple of years. Why don't we wait and let her decide what she wants. I just think ... please, leave her alone for now? I hope I haven't ... Think of her that's all. I'll see myself out.

CHRISSY leaves.

AGNES: So that's the end of it then.

THERESA: Not quite yet.

EXT. HOUSE—DAY

The next day. AGNES, THERESA and LOUISE are leaving the house and getting into the old sedan.

INT. CAR—DAY

AGNES watches out the passenger window as the car winds its way through a subdivision of large homes on large well-manicured lots.

EXT. SUBDIVISION—DAY

The sedan pulls into the driveway of one of the large well-manicured lots upon which sits one of the large homes.

INT. KEN AND VALERIE'S LIVING ROOM—DAY

A living room that's trying too hard. A large window looks out onto the subdivision of homes and well-manicured lawns. A fireplace unused and painted white dominates the room. Above the fireplace white wicker wreaths hang on either side of a gold-framed mirror. A neutral-coloured carpet lies under a large, loud, uncomfortable sofa and matching armchair. Pots of pot-pourri sit on colonial-style tables, framing a huge home entertainment centre. AGNES, THERESA and LOUISE, scrubbed and buttoned up, sit uncomfortably and in silence, the only sound comes from ice cubes clinking in LOUISE's glass of cola.

LOUISE: (*whispering*) I wanna go home.

THERESA: Drink your pop.

AGNES looks at her watch.

LOUISE: I wanna go home.

AGNES: Drink your pop.

VALERIE enters the room. She is a tiny woman in her mid-30s but she dresses and acts like she's 20. Today she is dressed as if for an important occasion.

VALERIE: Is everybody okay, can I get anybody anything?

THERESA: Oh no everything's great thanks Valerie.

AGNES: Is he going to be much longer?

VALERIE: The potatoes are almost ready, then we'll get
him his sweater and he'll be down.

VALERIE leaves the room.

THERESA: (*to AGNES*) Be nice.

AGNES: Why?

LOUISE: I wanna—

AGNES and THERESA: Drink your pop.

INT. KEN AND VALERIE'S KITCHEN—DAY

*Later. In the kitchen which is decoratively reminiscent of
the living room, AGNES, THERESA and LOUISE sit stiffly
around the table. Two empty chairs await the arrival of
VALERIE and KEN, the sisters' father. The food sits
cooling on the table. LOUISE still nurses her cola. AGNES
looks at her watch. THERESA picks a bit of meat from a
serving plate. Sounds of VALERIE and KEN approaching.
The women turn, THERESA rises. They see their father
for the first time in ten years and he looks like he's aged
a hundred. Hunched over, shuffling and mumbling to
himself, lost in another world he approaches the table
aided by VALERIE. The three women watch him with
various levels of denial and incredulousness.*

THERESA: Dad?

KEN: This isn't the sweater with the blue butter on it?
This is the one with the other one isn't it?

VALERIE: Look who it is Ken. Look it's your girls Ken.

*KEN looks up and around at the three women for a
moment.*

KEN: Hello how are you?

LOUISE: Fine.

THERESA: Hello Dad.

KEN: Hello how are you?

THERESA: How are you Dad?

*VALERIE helps KEN into his chair. Everyone takes their
place at the table. KEN immediately begins to eat messily,*

food dribbling onto his chin. As if taking a cue the others start to eat. The three sisters try not to stare at their father.

VALERIE: (*to the sisters as if KEN can't hear*) You've got to kind of catch his eye to get his attention. His hearing and that—

KEN looks up at THERESA. THERESA motions to his chin, he does not notice. Without missing a beat as she speaks VALERIE wipes KEN's chin.

VALERIE: —you know. Anyway so sorry about your mom. But you know it's a blessing in the end isn't it. I mean she was sick for so long.

A beat while no one responds.

VALERIE: I thought we might make it to the funeral but it's hard to get out that much. Ken's really slowed down the last couple of years, he needs help all the time.

KEN points across the table to the dinner rolls.

KEN: Pass the binoculars.

VALERIE: The buns Ken.

VALERIE gets KEN a bun and butters it.

VALERIE: He gets mixed up and that eh, on just simple little words. It's funny, even sometimes like the phone will ring and he'll say "get the tub." I mean it's not funny really it's … You know.

KEN looks up at LOUISE. Slowly he reaches out to touch her face. As he reaches toward her LOUISE pulls back at the same rate. As KEN's hand approaches LOUISE's face he narrows his eyes and growls seductively. LOUISE closes her eyes and raises her shoulders as if his touch would burn.

AGNES: (*slamming her hand on the table*) Stop it!

KEN is startled by AGNES. VALERIE gently places a buttered bun on his plate.

VALERIE: Ken. Be good.

KEN: (*to AGNES*) Don't be mad. Are you mad at me? Don't be mad at me.

VALERIE: She's not mad at you Ken. Eat your bun.

Everyone eats in silence.

EXT. KEN AND VALERIE'S HOUSE—DUSK

Later. VALERIE, AGNES, THERESA and LOUISE descend the steps of the house and move toward the car. KEN stands at the door. AGNES hangs back a bit. VALERIE says her goodbyes to LOUISE and THERESA as they get in the car. AGNES returns to KEN who has moved to the edge of the steps. She stands on the ground below her father, she looks up into his face. She speaks quietly, pointedly.

AGNES: I'm going to turn around, and I'm going to walk away, and when I walk away, I'm finally walking away from you.

KEN smiles at her.

KEN: Are we going swimming? It's a bit woolly. Are we going swimming?

AGNES walks away.

KEN: (*calling after*) Bye bye.

INT. KITCHEN—NIGHT

The three women enter the dark kitchen and turn on the lights. Without even taking off their coats THERESA starts to make tea and LOUISE and AGNES sit at the table silently. After a few moments THERESA begins to laugh.

AGNES: What?

THERESA: Pass the binoculars.

AGNES: I know.

AGNES can't help but laugh as well.

THERESA: Pass the binoculars.

AGNES: Pass the binoculars and get the tub.

THERESA: The tub! I know! The tub! So the tub's the phone then is it and the phone's the tub?

AGNES and THERESA laugh.

LOUISE: Well those binoculars were so tough they could've used a good soak in the phone.

All three women laugh.

THERESA: Honest to God!

THE CAMERA drifts toward the ceiling. As the women continue to talk and laugh.

AGNES: (*o.c.*) And he's probably out in their backyard watching birds with his buns.

The women erupt in gales of laughter.

DISSOLVE TO:

INT. ROSE'S BEDROOM—NIGHT

THE CAMERA drifts through the floor and up through ROSE's room, now empty, the bed neatly made, the curtains blowing lightly against the night breeze, the stars outside the window, the sisters' laughter rising through the ceiling and into the sky.

INT. LOUISE AND AGNES'S ROOM—NIGHT

Later. A dim light on AGNES's bedside table glows as AGNES undresses. LOUISE is already in bed, lying awake, staring at the ceiling.

AGNES: Are you all right.

LOUISE: I'm all right. Are you?

AGNES: Yeah.

LOUISE: Agnes?

AGNES: Yeah?

LOUISE: I think there's something I want.

AGNES: What?

LOUISE: It seems like maybe it's too much to want.

AGNES: What is it?

LOUISE: (*not wanting to say*) I don't know.

AGNES: Is it something to do with Dory?

LOUISE: Shh.

AGNES: Is it?

LOUISE: Yeah.

AGNES: I think I know what it is.

LOUISE: Yeah?

AGNES: Yeah.

LOUISE: I think it's what I want.

AGNES: Are you sure?

LOUISE: Yeah.

AGNES: Then that's what you should do.

LOUISE: Theresa wouldn't like it.

AGNES: It has nothing to do with Theresa. Theresa will get over it.

LOUISE: Okay.

AGNES: At least one of us should get what we want.

A knock on the front door. Both women turn toward the sound.

INT. LIVING ROOM—NIGHT

LOUISE moves the small chair which sits in front of the unused front door. AGNES stands behind her in the kitchen. THERESA enters from upstairs in her night clothes.

THERESA: What's going on?

LOUISE: Somebody's at the front door.

THERESA: Who is it?

LOUISE looks out the window of the door.

LOUISE: I don't know.

THERESA: Tell them to go around the side.

LOUISE: I don't know who it is.

LOUISE pulls at the door which is stuck, with some difficulty LOUISE manages to get the door open. THERESA and AGNES wait and watch.

LOUISE: Hello?

JOANIE: (*o.c.*) Is Carmel home?

LOUISE: Who?

THERESA looks at AGNES. AGNES steps into the room and sees JOANIE on the front step.

JOANIE: (*to AGNES*) Hi. It's freezing.

INT. KITCHEN/LIVING ROOM—NIGHT

JOANIE sits at the table with a glass of milk and some sweet squares before her. LOUISE sits at the table with her. THERESA hovers near the sink. AGNES is on the phone.

AGNES: (*on phone*) Yes she's fine … She's fine … We're leaving shortly … No she's fine … She's just having a glass of milk … We'll be half an hour …

LOUISE: Do you want to watch TV?

JOANIE: No thanks.

LOUISE: We get seventy-five channels.

JOANIE: But there's still never anything on.

LOUISE: No I know.

While at the sink THERESA opens the drawer where she put the picture of AGNES as a girl. She takes out the picture.

LOUISE: Do you play any instruments?

JOANIE: No.

LOUISE: Do you like bowling?

JOANIE: I never bowled.

LOUISE: You never bowled. Oh bowling's great.

JOANIE: They don't have bowling at home.

LOUISE: Too bad. I like your hair.

JOANIE: Thanks.

LOUISE: You want some more milk?

JOANIE: Okay.

LOUISE: Theresa she wants some more milk.

JOANIE looks questioningly up at "Camille."

JOANIE: I thought you were Camille?

LOUISE: Who's Camille?

THERESA comes to the table and pours JOANIE some more milk. She places the photograph before JOANIE.

THERESA: That's for you.

JOANIE: Who is it?

THERESA: Carmel.

LOUISE: Who's Carmel?

INT. CAR—NIGHT

AGNES and JOANIE drive silently along the dark highway taking JOANIE back to CHRISSY's.

JOANIE: Your real name's not Carmel is it.

AGNES: No.

JOANIE: Is it Angie?

AGNES: Agnes.

JOANIE: Agnes?

AGNES: Agnes. Angie.

EXT. TOWN MAIN STREET—NIGHT

The sedan idles across the street from the craft shop.

INT. CAR—NIGHT

JOANIE and AGNES sit in the car. CHRISSY comes out and stands on the step of the craft shop.

JOANIE: I finished the end of *Jane Eyre.*

AGNES: Did you like it?

JOANIE: Not really.

AGNES: Me neither.

JOANIE opens the door. She turns back and looks at AGNES.

JOANIE: Are you my mother?

AGNES: (*indicating CHRISSY across the street*) She's your mother.

JOANIE: What's my real name?

AGNES: Joanie.

JOANIE: Really?

AGNES nods yes. JOANIE gets out of the car and goes to CHRISSY. CHRISSY hugs her and takes her inside. CHRISSY looks over and waves thanks at AGNES. AGNES waves back.

INT. KITCHEN—DAY

AGNES stands in the window smoking, waiting for LOUISE. THERESA makes sandwiches which she places in a basket on the counter all the while keeping watch out the back door for LOUISE. AGNES calls to THERESA that someone's coming. THERESA comes over to look.

EXT. HOUSE—DAY

DORY's red truck pulls up in front of the house with LOUISE in the driver's seat. LOUISE bounds out of the truck. AGNES and THERESA, with the basket, walk down the front lawn to meet LOUISE. LOUISE struts around the truck.

THERESA: What the heck is this?

LOUISE: It's our new car.

THERESA: It's not a car it's a truck.

LOUISE: Isn't she beautiful?

THERESA: Where'd you get it in your head to do this?

LOUISE: Agnes told me to. I told her you wouldn't like it but she said you'd get over it.

AGNES: Did she?

AGNES: (*to THERESA*) I guess I did.

> *THERESA looks on disbelievingly. LOUISE puts THERESA's basket in the back. AGNES gets in. LOUISE has to practically beg then force THERESA to get in.*

EXT. HIGHWAY—DRIVING

The truck is driving out along the highway. We follow it along from above until it speeds out past us and away.

EXT. BEACH—DAY

The truck sits near the sand at the edge of the beach. AGNES, THERESA and LOUISE carefully step down the rocky bank which leads to the beach. THERESA carries the basket of food as the three sisters stand on a small knoll some distance from the water looking down the beach. JOANIE comes out of the water and stands on the beach beside CHRISSY who sits on a blanket on the beach. JOANIE waves at the three women. The sisters wave back and make their way across the beach for a family picnic. THE CAMERA pulls out and away across the endless beach, the water, the impossibly blue sky.

CREDITS